Addressing Special Educational Needs and Disability in the Curriculum: Maths

The SEND Code of Practice (2015) reinforced the requirement that all teachers must meet the needs of all learners. This topical book provides practical, tried and tested strategies and resources that will support teachers in making maths lessons accessible and interesting for all pupils, including those with special needs. The author draws on a wealth of experience to share his understanding of special educational needs and disabilities and show how the maths teacher can reduce or remove any barriers to learning.

Offering strategies that are specific to the context of maths teaching, this book will enable teachers to:

- adopt a 'problem-solving' approach to ensure students use and apply mathematics at all times during their learning
- develop students' understanding of mathematical ideas
- structure lessons to empower and actively engage students
- create a mutually supportive classroom which maximises learning opportunities
- plan the classroom layout and displays to enhance learning, for example displaying number lines, vocabulary lists and pupils' work
- successfully train and fully use the support of their teaching assistants.

An invaluable tool for continuing professional development, this text will be essential for secondary maths teachers (and their teaching assistants) seeking guidance specific to teaching maths to all pupils, regardless of their individual needs. The book will also be of interest to secondary SENCOs, senior management teams and ITT providers.

In addition to free online resources, a range of appendices provide maths teachers with a variety of pro forma and activity sheets to support effective teaching. This is an essential tool for maths teachers and teaching assistants, and will help to deliver successful, inclusive lessons for all pupils.

Max Wallace is Lead Practitioner for Maths at King Edward VI Community College, Devon, UK.

Addressing Special Educational Needs and Disability in the Curriculum

Series editor: Linda Evans

Children and young people with a diverse range of special educational needs and disabilities (SEND) are expected to access the full curriculum. Crucially, the current professional standards make it clear that *every* teacher must take responsibility for *all* pupils in their classes. Titles in this fully revised and updated series will be essential for teachers seeking subject-specific guidance on meeting their pupils' individual needs. In line with recent curriculum changes, the new Code of Practice for SEN and other pedagogical developments, these titles provide clear, practical strategies and resources that have proved to be effective and successful in their particular subject area. Written by practitioners, they can be used by departmental teams and in 'whole-school' training sessions as professional development resources. With free Web-based online resources also available to complement the books, these resources will be an asset to any teaching professional helping to develop policy and provision for learners with SEND.

The new national curriculum content will prove challenging for many learners, and teachers of children in Y5 and Y6 will also find the books a valuable resource.

Titles in this series include:

Addressing Special Educational Needs and Disability in the Curriculum: Modern Foreign Languages
John Connor

Addressing Special Educational Needs and Disability in the Curriculum: Music
Victoria Jaquiss and Diane Paterson

Addressing Special Educational Needs and Disability in the Curriculum: PE and Sport
Crispin Andrews

Addressing Special Educational Needs and Disability in the Curriculum: Science
Marion Frankland

Addressing Special Educational Needs and Disability in the Curriculum: Design and Technology
Louise T. Davies

Addressing Special Educational Needs and Disability in the Curriculum: History
Ian Luff and Richard Harris

Addressing Special Educational Needs and Disability in the Curriculum: Religious Education
Dilwyn Hunt

Addressing Special Educational Needs and Disability in the Curriculum: Geography
Graeme Eyre

Addressing Special Educational Needs and Disability in the Curriculum: Art
Gill Curry and Kim Earle

Addressing Special Educational Needs and Disability in the Curriculum: English
Tim Hurst

Addressing Special Educational Needs and Disability in the Curriculum: Maths
Max Wallace

Addressing Special Educational Needs and Disability in the Curriculum: Maths

Second edition

Max Wallace

Routledge
Taylor & Francis Group

LONDON AND NEW YORK

Second edition published 2018
by Routledge
2 Park Square, Milton Park, Abingdon, Oxon OX14 4RN

and by Routledge
711 Third Avenue, New York, NY 10017

Routledge is an imprint of the Taylor & Francis Group, an informa business

First edition published 2004 by David Fulton Publishers as *Meeting SEN in the Curriculum: Maths* by Brian Sharp

British Library Cataloguing in Publication Data
A catalogue record for this book is available from the British Library

Library of Congress Cataloging in Publication Data
A catalog record for this book has been requested

ISBN: 978-1-138-28339-8 (hbk)
ISBN: 978-1-138-28340-4 (pbk)
ISBN: 978-1-315-27029-6 (ebk)

Typeset in Helvetica
by Keystroke, Neville Lodge, Tettenhall, Wolverhampton

Visit eResources: www.routledge.com/9781138283404

Contents

Appendices

Series authors

The author

Max Wallace has nine years' experience of teaching children with special educational needs. He currently works as an advanced skills teacher at an inclusive mainstream secondary school. Appointed as a specialist leader in education for mathematics, Max mentors and coaches teachers in a wide network of schools. He has previously worked as a head of year and was responsible for the continuing professional development of colleagues. He has a doctorate in mathematics from Cardiff University.

A dedicated team of SEND specialists and subject specialists have contributed to this series:

Series editor

Linda D. Evans was commissioning editor for the original books in this series and has coordinated the updating process for these new editions. She has taught children of all ages over the years and posts have included those of SENCO, LA adviser, Ofsted inspector and HE tutor/lecturer. She was awarded a PhD in 2000 following research on improving educational outcomes for children (primary and secondary). Since then, Linda has been commissioning editor for David Fulton Publishing (SEN) as well as editor of a number of educational journals and newsletters; she has also written books, practical classroom resources, Master's course materials and school improvement guidance. She maintains her contact with school practitioners through her work as a part-time ITT tutor and educational consultant.

SEND specialist

Sue Briggs has been supporting the education and inclusion of children with special educational needs and disabilities and their parents for over 20 years, variously as teacher, Ofsted inspector, specialist member of the SEN and Disability Tribunal, school improvement partner, consultant and adviser. She holds a Master's degree in education, a first class BEd and a diploma in special education (DPSE distinction). Sue was a national lead for the Achievement for All programme (2011–2013) and a regional adviser for the Early Support programme for the Council for Disabled Children (2014–2015) and is currently an independent education and leadership consultant. Sue is the author of several specialist books and publications including *Meeting SEND in Primary Classrooms* and *Meeting SEND in Secondary Classrooms* (Routledge, 2015).

Subject specialists

Art

Gill Curry was head of art in a secondary school in Wirral for 20 years and advisory teacher for art and gifted and talented strand coordinator. She has an MA in print from the University of Chester and an MA in women's studies from the University of Liverpool. She is a practising artist specialising in print and exhibits nationally and internationally, running courses regularly in schools and print studios.

Kim Earle is vice principal at Birkenhead High School Academy for Girls on the Wirral. She has previously been a head of art and head of creative arts, securing Artsmark Gold in all the establishments in which she has worked. Kim was also formerly able pupils and arts consultant in St Helens, working across special schools and mainstream schools with teaching and support staff on art policy and practice. She still teaches art in a mixed ability setting in her current school and works closely with local schools and outside organisations to address barriers to learning.

Design and technology

Louise T. Davies is founder of the Food Teachers Centre offering advice and guidance to the DfE and other organisations based on her years of experience as a teacher and teacher trainer, and her role in curriculum development at QCA and the Royal College of Art. She led innovation at the Design and Technology Association, providing expertise for a range of curriculum and CPD programmes and specialist advice on teaching standards and best practice, including meeting special educational needs. Most recently, she has worked as lead consultant for the School Food Champions programme (2013–2016) and as an adviser to the DfE on the new GCSE in food preparation and nutrition.

English

Tim Hurst began his career as an English teacher at the Willian School in Hertfordshire, becoming Second in English before deciding that his future lay in SEND. He studied for an advanced diploma in special educational needs and has been a SEN coordinator in five schools in Hertfordshire, Essex and Suffolk. Tim has always been committed to the concept of inclusion and is particularly interested in reading development, which he passionately believes in as a whole-school responsibility.

Geography

Graeme Eyre has considerable experience of teaching and leading geography in secondary schools in a range of different contexts, and is currently Assistant Principal for Intervention at an academy in inner London. Graeme is a consultant to the Geographical Association and a Fellow of the Royal Geographical Society. He has also delivered training and CPD for teachers at all levels. He holds a BA in geography, a PGCE in secondary geography and an MA in geography education.

History

Ian Luff retired as deputy headteacher of Kesgrave High School in 2013 after a 32-year career during which he had been head of history in four comprehensive schools and an advisory teacher with the London Borough of Barking and Dagenham. He is an honorary fellow of the Historical Association and currently works as an associate tutor on the PGCE history course at the University of East Anglia and as a consultant in history education.

Richard Harris has been teaching since 1989. He has taught in three comprehensive schools, as history teacher, head of department and head of faculty. He has also worked as teacher consultant for secondary history in West Berkshire. Since 2001 he has been involved in history initial teacher education, firstly at the University of Southampton and more recently at the University of Reading. He has also worked extensively with the Historical Association and Council of Europe in the areas of history education and teacher training, and has been made an honorary fellow of the Historical Association. He is currently associate professor in history education and director of teaching and learning at the Institute of Education, University of Reading.

Languages

John Connor is a former head of faculty, local authority adviser and senior examiner. He has also served as an Ofsted team inspector for modern languages and special educational needs in mainstream settings. John was also an assessor on the Advanced Skills Teacher programme for the DfE. He is currently working as a trainer, author and consultant, and has directed teaching and learning quality audits across England, the Channel Islands, Europe, the Middle East and the Far East. He is also a governor of a local primary school.

Music

Victoria Jaquiss, FRSA, trained as a teacher of English and drama and held posts of English teacher, head of PSE, music and expressive arts at Foxwood School. She became a recognised authority on behaviour management and inclusion with children in challenging circumstances. The second half of her career has involved working for the Leeds Music Service/Leeds ArtForms as steel pan development officer and deputy inclusion manager/teacher. She was awarded the fellowship of the Royal Society of Arts in 2002.

Diane Paterson began teaching as a mainstream secondary music teacher. She went on to study how music technology could enable people with severe physical difficulties to make their own music, joining the Drake Music project in Yorkshire and becoming its regional leader. She then became inclusion manager/teacher at Leeds Music Service/ArtForms, working with children with additional needs. As secretary of YAMSEN: SpeciallyMusic, she now runs specialist regional workshops, music days and concerts for students with special/ additional needs and their carers.

PE and sport

Crispin Andrews is a qualified teacher and sports coach, and has worked extensively in Buckinghamshire schools coaching cricket and football and developing opportunities for girls in these two sports. He is currently a sports journalist, writing extensively for a wide range of educational journals, including *Special Children* and the *Times Educational Supplement*, and other publications such as *Cricket World*.

Religious education

Dilwyn Hunt taught RE for 18 years before becoming an adviser first in Birmingham and then in Dudley. He currently works as an independent RE adviser supporting local authorities, SACREs and schools. He is also in demand across the country as a speaker on all aspects of teaching RE, in both mainstream and special settings. He is the author of numerous popular classroom resources and books and currently serves as the executive assistant at the Association of RE Inspectors, Advisers and Consultants.

Science

Marion Frankland, CSciTeach, has been teaching for 16 years and was an advanced skills teacher of science. She has extensive experience of teaching science at all levels, in both mainstream and special schools, and has worked as a SENCO in a special school, gaining her qualification alongside her teaching commitments.

A few words from the series editor

The original version of this book formed part of the 'Meeting SEN in the Curriculum' series which was published ten years ago to much acclaim. The series won a BERA (British Educational Resources Award) and has been widely used by ITT providers, their students and trainees, curriculum and SEN advisers, department heads and teachers of all levels of experience. It has proven to be highly successful in helping to develop policy and provision for learners with special educational needs or disabilities.

The series was born out of an understanding that practitioners want information and guidance about improving teaching and learning that is *relevant to them* – rooted in their particular subject, and applicable to pupils they encounter. These books exactly fulfil that function.

Those original books have stood the test of time in many ways – their tried and tested, practical strategies are as relevant and effective as ever. Legislation and national guidance have moved on, however, as have resources and technology; new terminology accompanies all of these changes. For example, we have changed the series title to incorporate the acronym 'SEND' (special educational needs and disability) which has been adopted in official documents and in many schools in response to recent legislation and the revised Code of Practice. The important point to make is that our authors have addressed the needs of pupils with a wide range of special or 'additional' needs; some will have educational, health and care (EHC) plans which have replaced 'statements', but most will not. Some will have identified 'syndromes' or 'conditions' but many will simply be termed 'low attainers', pupils who, for whatever reason, do not easily make progress.

This second edition encompasses recent developments in education, and specifically in the teaching of mathematics. At the time of publication, education is still very much in an era of change; our national curriculum, monitoring and assessment systems are all newly fashioned and many schools are still adjusting to changes and developing their own ways forward. The ideas and guidance contained in this book, however, transcend the fluctuations of national politics and policy and provide a framework for ensuring that pupils with SEND can 'enjoy and achieve' in their maths lessons.

NB: The term 'parent' is used throughout and is intended to cover any adult who is a child's main care-giver.

Linda D. Evans

Acknowledgements

Brian Sharp was the author of the first edition of this book (*Meeting SEN in the Curriculum: Maths*, 2004) and acknowledged a number of friends and colleagues who inspired and supported his writing, including staff at Cedar School in Southampton, Ludlow CE School, and Kingstone High School in Herefordshire.

Max Wallace would like to thank Emily and Arlo for their never ending support and encouragement.

The author and publishers of this second edition would like to thank:

David Evans of Fox Lane Photography

Staff and pupils of St John's CoE Middle School in Bromsgrove and Queensbury School in Erdington for allowing us to use their photographs.

Introduction

Ours to teach

Your class: thirty individuals to teach – to encourage, motivate and inspire: thirty individuals who must be seen to make good progress regardless of their various abilities, backgrounds, interests and personalities. This is what makes teaching so interesting!

> **Jason** demonstrates very little interest in school. He rarely completes homework and frequently turns up without a pen. He finds it hard to listen when you're talking and is likely to start his own conversation with a classmate. His work is untidy and mostly incomplete. It's difficult to find evidence of his progress this year.

> **Zoe** tries very hard in lessons but is slow to understand explanations and has difficulty in expressing herself. She has been assessed as having poor communication skills but there is no additional resourcing for her.

> **Ethan** is on the autistic spectrum and finds it difficult to relate to other people, to work in a group and to understand social norms. He has an education, health and care plan which provides for some TA support but this is not timetabled for all lessons.

Do you recognise these youngsters? Our school population is now more diverse than ever before, with pupils of very different abilities, aptitudes and interests, from a wide range of cultures, making up our mainstream and special school classes. Many of these learners will experience difficulties of some sort at school, especially when they are faced with higher academic expectations at the end of KS2 and into KS3–4.

Whether they have a specific special educational need like dyslexia, or are on the autistic spectrum, or for various reasons cannot conform to our behavioural expectations – *they are ours to teach*. Our lessons must ensure that each and every pupil can develop their skills and knowledge and make good progress.

How can this book help?

The information, ideas and guidance in this book will enable teachers of mathematics (and their teaching assistants) to plan and deliver lessons that will meet the individual needs of learners who experience difficulties. It will be especially valuable to maths teachers because the ideas and guidance are provided within a subject context, ensuring relevance and practicability.

Teachers who cater well for pupils with special educational needs and disabilities (SEND) are likely to cater well for *all* pupils – demonstrating outstanding practice in their everyday teaching. These teachers have a keen awareness of the many factors affecting a pupil's ability to learn, not only characteristics of the individual but also aspects of the learning environment that can either help or hinder learning. This book will help practitioners to develop strategies that can be used selectively to enable each and every learner to make progress.

Professional development

Our education system is constantly changing. The national curriculum, SEND legislation, examination reform and significant change to Ofsted inspection mean that teachers need to keep up to date and be able to develop the knowledge, skills and understanding necessary to meet the needs of all the learners they teach. High-quality continuing professional development (CPD) has a big part to play in this.

Faculties and subject teams planning for outstanding teaching and learning should consider how they regularly review and improve their provision by:

- auditing:

    a) the skills and expertise of current staff (teachers and assistants);
    b) their professional development needs for SEND, based on the current cohorts of pupils;

    (An audit pro forma can be found in the eResources at: www.routledge.com/9781138283404)

- using the information from the two audits to develop a CPD programme (using internal staff, colleagues from nearby schools and/or consultants to deliver bespoke training);

- enabling teachers to observe each other, teach together, visit other classrooms and other schools;
- encouraging staff to reflect on their practice and feel comfortable in sharing both the positive and the negative experiences;
- establishing an ethos that values everyone's expertise (including pupils and parents who might be able to contribute to training sessions);
- using online resources that are readily available to support workforce development (e.g. www.nasen.org.uk/resources);
- encouraging staff to access (and disseminate) further study and high-quality professional development.

This book, and the others in the series, will be invaluable in contributing to whole-school CPD on meeting special educational needs, and in facilitating subject-specific staff development within departments.

1 Meeting special educational needs and disabilities

Your responsibility

New legislation and national guidance in 2014 changed the landscape of educational provision for pupils with any sort of 'additional' or 'special' needs. The vast majority of learners, including those with 'moderate' or 'mild' learning difficulties, weak communication skills, dyslexia or social/behavioural needs, rarely attract additional resources; they are very much accepted as part of the 'mainstream mix'. Pupils with more significant special educational needs and/or disabilities (SEND) may have an education, health and care plan (EHC plan): this outlines how particular needs will be met, often involving professionals from different disciplines, and sometimes specifying adult support in the classroom. Both groups of pupils are ultimately the responsibility of the class teacher, whether in mainstream or special education.

High quality teaching that is differentiated and personalised will meet the individual needs of the majority of children and young people. Some children and young people need educational provision that is additional to or different from this. This is special educational provision under Section 21 of the Children and Families Act 2014. Schools and colleges **must** use their best endeavours to ensure that such provision is made for those who need it. Special educational provision is underpinned by high quality teaching and is compromised by anything less.

SEND Code of Practice (DfE 2015)

There is more information about legislation (the Children and Families Act 2014; the Equality Act 2010) and guidance (SEND Code of Practice) in Appendix 1.

Definition of SEND

A pupil has special educational needs if he or she:

- has a significantly greater difficulty in learning than the majority of others of the same age; or
- has a disability which prevents or hinders him or her from making use of facilities of a kind generally provided for others of the same age in mainstream schools or mainstream post-16 institutions.

(SEND Code of Practice 2015)

The SEND Code of Practice identifies four broad areas of SEND, but remember that this gives only an overview of the range of needs that should be planned for by schools; pupils' needs rarely fit neatly into one area of need only.

Whole-school ethos

Successful schools are proactive in identifying and addressing pupils' special needs, focusing on adapting the educational context and environment rather than on 'fixing' an individual learner. Adapting systems and teaching programmes rather than trying to force the pupil to conform to rigid expectations will lead to a greater chance of success in terms of learning outcomes. Guidance on whole-school and departmental policy making can be found in

Table 1.1 The four broad areas of SEND

Communication and interaction	Cognition and learning	Social, emotional and mental health difficulties	Sensory and/or physical needs
Speech, language and communication needs (SLCN)	Specific learning difficulties (SpLD)	Mental health difficulties such as anxiety or depression, self-harming, substance abuse or eating disorders	Vision impairment (VI)
Asperger's Syndrome and Autism (ASD)	Moderate learning difficulties (MLD)		Hearing impairment (HI)
			Multi-sensory impairment (MSI)
	Severe learning difficulties (SLD)	Attention deficit disorders, attention deficit hyperactivity disorder or attachment disorder	
			Physical disability (PD)
	Profound and multiple learning difficulties (PMLD)		

Appendix 2 and a sample departmental policy for SEND can be downloaded from www.routledge.com/9781138283404.

Policy into practice

In many cases, pupils' individual learning needs will be met through differentiation of tasks and materials in their lessons; sometimes this will be supplemented by targeted interventions such as literacy 'catch-up' programmes delivered outside the classroom. A smaller number of pupils may need access to more specialist equipment and approaches, perhaps based on advice and support from external specialists.

The main thrust of the Children and Families Act and Chapter 6 of the SEND Code of Practice is that outcomes for pupils with SEND must be improved and that schools and individual teachers must have high aspirations and expectations for all.

In practice, this means that pupils should be enabled to:

- **achieve their best**; additional provision made for pupils with SEND will enable them to make accelerated progress so that the gap in progress and attainment between them and other pupils is reduced. Being identified with SEND should no longer be a reason for a pupil making less than good progress.
- **become confident individuals living fulfilling lives**; if you ask parents of children with SEND what is important to them for their child's future, they often answer 'happiness, the opportunity to achieve his or her potential, friendships and a loving family' – just what we all want for our children. Outcomes in terms of well-being, social skills and growing independence are equally as important as academic outcomes for children and young people with SEND.
- **make a successful transition into adulthood, whether into employment, further or higher education or training;** decisions made at transition from primary school, in Year 7 and beyond should be made in the context of preparation for adulthood. For example, where a pupil has had full-time support from a teaching assistant in primary school, the secondary school's first reaction might be to continue this level of support after transition. This may result in long-term dependency on adults, however, or limited opportunities to develop social skills, both of which impact negatively on preparation for adulthood.

Excellent classroom provision

Later chapters provide lots of subject-specific ideas and guidance on strategies to support pupils with SEND. In Appendix 3 you will find useful checklists to help you support pupils with identified 'conditions', but there are some generic approaches that form the foundations of outstanding provision, such as:

- providing support from adults or other pupils;
- adapting tasks or environments;
- using specialist aids and equipment as appropriate.

The starting points listed below provide a sound basis for creating an inclusive learning environment that will benefit *all* pupils, while being especially important for those with SEND.

Develop pupils' understanding through the use of all available senses by:

- using resources that pupils can access through sight *and* sound (and where appropriate also use the senses of touch, taste and smell to broaden understanding and ensure stronger memory);
- regularly employing resources such as symbols, pictures and film to increase pupils' knowledge of the wider world and contextualise new information and skills;
- encouraging and enabling pupils to take part in activities such as play, drama, class visits and exploring the environment.

Help pupils to learn effectively and prepare for further or higher education, work or training by:

- setting realistic demands within high expectations;
- using positive strategies to manage behaviour;
- giving pupils opportunities and encouragement to develop the skills to work effectively in a group or with a partner;
- teaching all pupils to value and respect the contribution of others;
- encouraging independent working skills;
- teaching essential safety rules.

Help pupils to develop communication skills, language and literacy by:

- making sure all pupils can see your face when you are speaking;
- giving clear, step-by-step instructions, and limiting the amount of information given at one time;
- providing a list of key vocabulary for each lesson;

- choosing texts that pupils can read and understand;
- making texts available in different formats, including large text or symbols, or by using screen-reader programs;
- putting headings and important points in bold or highlighting to make them easier to scan;
- presenting written information as concisely as possible, using bullet points, images or diagrams.

Support pupils with disabilities by:

- encouraging pupils to be as independent as possible;
- enabling them to work with other, non-disabled pupils;
- making sure the classroom environment is suitable, e.g. uncluttered space to facilitate movement around the classroom or lab; adapted resources that are labelled and accessible;
- being aware that some pupils will take longer to complete tasks, including homework;
- taking into account the higher levels of concentration and physical exertion required by some pupils (even in activities such as reading and writing) that will lead to increased fatigue for pupils who may already have reduced stamina;
- being aware of the extra effort required by some pupils to follow oral work, whether through the use of residual hearing, lip reading or signed support, and of the tiredness and limited concentration which is likely to ensue;
- ensuring all pupils are included, and can participate safely, in school trips and off-site visits.

These and other more specific strategies are placed in the context of supporting particular individuals such as those described in the case studies in Chapter 6.

2 The inclusive mathematics classroom

Any system of education . . . that diminishes the school's role in nurturing its pupils' self-esteem fails at one of its primary functions.

(Bruner 1996)

Inclusion, empowerment and self-esteem

A positive self-esteem is an essential requirement for effective learning and if 'the project of inclusion is a political and social struggle to enable the valuing of difference and identity' (Corbett and Slee 2000), then our classrooms become the central stage for this process of valuing all pupils. We do this by valuing their contributions to the community – the classroom – that we manage.

An inclusive mathematics classroom must be centrally concerned with empowerment and the building of self-esteem in all pupils. The teacher in this classroom focuses on problem-solving activities and promotes a conjecturing atmosphere to enable all pupils to discuss and explore ideas.

Problem-solving

A problem-solving approach to learning, where pupils are using and applying mathematics is an essential feature of an inclusive classroom. The latest KS2, KS3 and KS4 curriculums explicitly identify problem-solving as an aim/ assessment objective and as Prestage and Perks (2001) suggest: '"Using and Applying Mathematics" should be integrated into the mathematics curriculum as much as possible. It is not an add-on: it describes a way of working mathematically.'

We can consider two aspects of the problem-solving classroom:

- The pupils are empowered and actively engaged in solving problems, together, independently or with support.

- The teacher (and other professionals who share the classroom) are actively engaged in solving the problems of how children will learn through given objectives.

In order to develop all pupils' self-esteem, and for the group to engage fully in discussions about solving problems together, we must create a classroom climate for learning that encourages these features. According to Carol Dweck (2007), helping students adopt a growth mindset will enable them to believe that their ability is not fixed, and that their improvement is related to hard work and them adopting good strategies. Assuming the presence of such belief, John Mason (1988) argues that 'mathematical thinking is best supported by adopting a conjecturing attitude' and Greeno *et al.* (1997) assert that, 'in constructing meaning in mathematics, we formulate and evaluate conjectures [and] build models'. The most effective classrooms are those where the children are engaged in constructing meaning in a 'mutually supportive' working environment. This does not happen by accident – cooperation can be taught; appreciating each other's contributions can be an explicit classroom value, and children can learn that allowing each other time to work things through is important for everyone. Children in these classrooms, therefore, carry a responsibility not only for their own learning, but also for everyone.

When a class is highly diverse in terms of achievement and social behaviour, creating an inclusive classroom is probably the greatest challenge we face. However, if we create this atmosphere for learning, it also becomes our greatest ally.

The inclusive mathematics classroom:

- empowers its pupils;
- focuses on problem-solving;
- enjoys a conjecturing atmosphere, where discussion can flourish.

This chapter attempts to address these issues through planning, and the following chapters look at teaching and evaluating mathematics lessons.

Views of mathematics: longer-term aims

How would your pupils respond to the question: what do you learn in mathematics lessons?

Children's answers invariably include examples of specific skills such as 'addition', 'times tables', 'angles', 'shapes', 'surveys', etc., but it is interesting to compare the responses of more able pupils with those who have difficulties with their mathematics. Often, the able pupil will tend to take a wider view of mathematics and will identify processes such as 'proof', 'generalising' and 'being systematic', and then one or two might also suggest attitudes – 'not giving up', 'checking our work to see if we're on the right lines', 'trying to explore ideas', 'seeing the problem in a different way'.

Many of these responses can be seen as aspects of achievement in mathematics, as illustrated in Table 2.1.

Answers in the second and third rows ('strategies for solving problems' and 'attitudes') rarely come from pupils who struggle with their mathematics. This analysis could highlight particular problems – either their own view of mathematics is limited, which could affect their learning, or they are only getting a diet of skills-based mathematics, without problem-solving contexts and explicit experience of the attitudes to mathematics and learning which are just as important. Their experience of mathematics is very likely to inform their view of it.

Table 2.1 Aspects of mathematical achievement

Aspect of mathematical achievement	*Example*
Fluency – skills and knowledge	Times tables, methods for calculating, using measuring tools
Strategies for solving problems	Organising and tabulating data, generalising, explaining, proving, checking work
Attitudes to learning mathematics, including metacognition	Persistence, wanting to ask 'What if . . .?', exploring ideas, checking how you are working

Many children with SEND not only have to face their own difficulties but low expectations too, whether their own or from their wider social experience. However, low expectations may be expressed in a number of ways in school too: from insufficient challenge, which does not acknowledge a need to develop strategies and attitudes as well as skills, or sometimes from being in an environment where the most vulnerable learners are also placed together with pupils with the most challenging behaviours. There are a variety of strategies we can undertake to overcome these issues. Some are illustrated in the section on managing classroom behaviour later in this chapter, and others, such as effective questioning, promoting collaboration and the use of formative assessment, will be discussed in later chapters.

All children learn best when they are clear about what it is they should achieve. If children have a narrow view of what they should learn in mathematics lessons, then the wider views and attitudes need to be made explicit. We are interested in solving problems and, in order to solve problems, we have to know about strategies such as collaboration. We also have to demonstrate the fact that although not all problems can be solved in five minutes, most can be solved with sustained effort.

Rogoff (1998) suggests that learning is a 'transformation of participation', and that a change in identity is the goal of learning. This can be likened to the distinction that we are teaching children to *become* mathematicians, rather than teaching them *about* mathematics. To participate in mathematical activities is to engage in the practices of, for instance, explaining, proving, generalising, being organised, hypothesising, reasoning and decision-making. None of these strategies evolve from doing pages of sums, or being taught a skill and then practising it without discussing its application.

Being taught to become a mathematician allows children a:

> sense of self, [which] in general, includes having various dispositions (habits of mind, predilections to view the world in particular ways), a certain kind of self-confidence and competence, and feelings of entitlement and empowerment.
>
> (Greeno *et al.* 1997)

Clearly, these considerations help us to clarify our longer-term aims for our children. This is an important distinction when we apply it to teaching children with SEND.

A vital aspect of being a mathematician is making decisions when solving problems. These decisions could be 'Which operation do I choose to solve this problem?' or 'How accurately do I need to measure this piece of wood?' or 'How should I present this information?' However, there is a common view that because children struggle with the *skills* involved in solving a problem, then the *decisions* about which skills to use, and when, and why, are assumed by the adults working with them, so that all that remains for the child is to make the calculations as instructed by the adult.

Here is a simple example. In an attempt to give children an experience in pie charts, a popular activity is to cut out a circle and fold it into quarters or eighths, and then children ask either four people or eight people a question about, for example, favourite breakfasts, and they colour in one segment for each person, thus completing a pie chart of 'favourite breakfasts'.

So, what if there are 12 people in the class? What hypothesis has been addressed through this activity, which necessitated a pie chart in the first place? Indeed, have the children learned *how* to use pie charts, *when* to use them, and *why*? All these decisions have been taken away from the activity – worse, taken away from the children, who have become little more than actors for a series of tasks devoid of the real stuff of mathematics. This practice is dis-empowering, not perhaps intentionally, but perhaps because it is predicated on a belief that children must 'have the skills first' and then, at some later date, make sense of them. (Although this clearly will not happen in this classroom, since they have not been offered the *experience* of making sense of the skills.)

There also seems to be a huge pressure to 'get the task done' or to reach the answer by the end of the lesson, but it is the *process* of getting to the answer that is the stuff of learning. Making mistakes along the way, meeting and overcoming problems, persisting, checking and reviewing our work are what mathematicians do, and children can act like mathematicians at any level of ability. A 2-year-old can generalise and distinguish between cows and sheep in a field; the person who claims not to be any good at mathematics yet finds the middle of a room by using a stick and a piece of string (applying a sound understanding of symmetry) might not recognise his or her natural use of mathematics.

This is not to say that developing technical fluency is unimportant, for as Greeno *et al.* continue: 'In constructing meaning in mathematics, we formulate and evaluate conjectures [and] build models . . . [For this] we must have the relevant mathematical tools at our disposal.'

The view that children should not be exposed to problem-solving until the skills are 'secure' means that they could then be presented with a diet of counting to 20 for years, with little room for other aspects of mathematics.

Expectations, progression, understanding

An understanding of inclusion also highlights expectations – of all those concerned with the children's learning, including the children themselves. The inclusion section of the National Curriculum in England Framework document (DfE 2013a) notes that 'teachers should set high expectations for every pupil' and 'they have a greater obligation to plan lessons for pupils who . . . come from disadvantaged backgrounds'. This should change our discourse about children with SEND from 'they can't do this' to 'they will have difficulties in achieving this, and so I need to plan to address these difficulties'.

For example, there are parents, pupils and professionals who claim that 'children with SEND can't do algebra', suggesting a deep misunderstanding of algebra *and what it is for*. The skills required to begin to think algebraically, e.g. considering relationships, understanding links and connections, should be within our expectations of entitlement for all pupils.

Children's expectations also have an impact on their own learning. Mason (1988) states: 'The pressure of new work is always present when studying mathematics, and it is compounded by the pressure, mounting to hopelessness and panic, of previous work only partly comprehended and insecure.' We can plan for accurate assessment (Chapter 4) and careful progression to help overcome this panic, but we should above all be planning for *understanding*.

There are some who may argue that we could give children a method that works, and they may come to understand it later.

Consider the example of multiplying numbers by ten, e.g.:

- $10 \times 2 = 20$
- $10 \times 9 = 90$
- $10 \times 16 = 160$

Many children make sense of this experience by suggesting that we add a zero. Many children take this view into adult life. Many teachers, assistants or other adults use it to help children see the pattern, and therefore multiplying by ten is down to adding nought. It is a method that works, but only in a limited context . . . What understanding of the process of multiplying by ten is happening here?

Consider these examples:

- $10 \times 2 = 20$
- *$10 \times 2.5 = ?$*
- $10 \times 3 = 30$

Many children answer $10 \times 2.5 = 2.50$, because they are doing just as they have been told. They add a zero. Some get further confused and offer $10 \times 2.5 = 20.5$, perhaps using the result $10 \times 2 = 20$ and realising that the answer ought to be bigger.

In teaching children a trick, like adding zero for multiplying by ten, we disempower them – keep them at a distance from genuine understanding of the number system and how it works. We fall into this trap perhaps from pressure of time and coverage, or perhaps because we see that it is difficult for some to understand and that completing the questions correctly has become the goal of the lesson rather than learning how to think mathematically.

Progression

For this reason, it is important to consider progression in developing children's understanding of mathematical ideas very carefully. Performance – P Scale (DfE 2014b), Mathematics Programmes of Study – Key Stages 1 and 2 (DfE 2013c) and Mathematics Programmes of Study – Key Stage 3 (DfE 2013b) can be used together for this purpose. The progression of objectives is identified for children working at P levels and for each year group (up to Year 6), and then in a broader format (Years 7–9 inclusive) after that.

Until the curriculum changed in 2013/14, it was possible to link together the previous versions of these documents – the National Strategy frameworks for primary (DfES 1999) and for Key Stage 3 (DfES 2001) and *Accessing the National Curriculum for Mathematics* (DfES 0292/2002) – to illustrate a clear line of progression for each mathematical objective. However, the new curriculum is purposely generic; it expects a teacher to understand how a topic develops in complexity and then plan a series of lessons building on their pupils' starting point. Should you not feel experienced/confident enough to do this, you should not be afraid of using the old documents to build up an idea of how a topic progresses, before checking them against the new curriculum to make sure you have covered everything necessary or not taught beyond the scope of the new curriculum.

It is worth noting that, when considering progression, one has to think as broadly as possible when it comes to considering what the prerequisite skills are for a particular objective. For example, Year 2 geometry requires children to 'Use mathematical vocabulary to describe position, direction and movement':

this is an early stage in understanding angles (as a measurement of turning) and a requisite for understanding how pie charts are constructed. The statistics section of the Mathematics Programmes of Study – Key Stage 3 (DfE 2013b) states: 'Pupils should be taught to construct and interpret tables, charts and diagrams', and therefore builds upon the earlier skills learned.

Through an activity designed in a problem-solving manner, children of all abilities can have opportunities to practise some of the skills relevant to their needs. More importantly, they are also working with a picture of how those particular skills are relevant and useful to the problem they are trying to solve. In trying to address the many different needs presented by a class of children, instead of 'individualised learning' that addresses the variety of learning objectives through several different contexts, a class could have one context that has multiple objectives. For example:

> Class 7B includes one child who has difficulties in counting, another needs practice in measuring accurately, others have difficulties in presenting their work, others may be poor at working collaboratively, some do not interpret diagrams and charts. The teacher devises a meaningful activity in data handling based on one of several different hypotheses, e.g. 'Boys have larger feet than girls' or 'Tall people have larger hands'. This involves a range of objectives, including counting, measuring, drawing diagrams, working in a team, interpreting each other's charts, as well as many others which meet with the idea of a community of mathematicians working together, e.g. a group presenting its results to others and trying to convince them that their data demonstrates that 'boys have bigger feet than girls', and justifying their choices in collecting certain types of data and presenting them in particular ways.

In this way, we do not start with the individual objectives at the level children appear to be working at, but instead look at the context from the higher-level objectives relevant to the year group and then devise activities that will meet the range of objectives for the children.

Classroom culture

Let us consider the problems encountered in developing good mathematics teaching at the same time as creating an effective learning environment.

The Special Educational Needs and Disability Code of Practice: 0 to 25 Years (DfE 2015) and the inclusion section of the National Curriculum in England: Framework for Key Stages 1 to 4 (DfE 2014c) state respectively:

- Teachers are responsible and accountable for the progress and development of the pupils in their class.
- Lessons should be planned to ensure there are no barriers to every pupil achieving.

Progress, development and achievement in mathematics include pupils learning the content in the national curriculum, and therefore it is reasonable to state that the teacher is responsible for creating a learning environment in which this curriculum can be met. The latest versions of the national curriculum for Key Stages 3 and 4 both include the assessment objective 'Reason Mathematically' (often referred to as AO2) and also an explicit spoken language section for the first time:

> They (pupils) must be assisted in making their thinking clear to themselves as well as others and teachers should ensure that pupils build secure foundations by using discussion to probe and remedy their misconceptions.

Clearly, the expectations are that for a significant part of lessons we conduct thoughtful, reflective discussions about the mathematics problems we are solving. However, the problem many of us face is that we are often dealing with children whose difficulties are complex and work against building a community of learners. Too common is the 'put-down' culture, where anyone successful is mocked, anyone who makes a public mistake is ridiculed, and some children cannot take turns or wait for others to answer but butt in and shout out. These attitudes inhibit learning in mathematics classrooms. It's not the answer we are working for – it is learning how to solve problems. That takes thinking, and thinking takes time.

Mason (1988) stresses that 'an attitude or atmosphere of conjecturing frees you from the dreadful fear of being wrong . . . we should bless our mistakes as golden opportunities'. Learning from mistakes is valid learning – as Mason continues: 'Being right lessens the opportunity to modify and learn.'

Sometimes we are well intentioned by trying to reduce the scope for children with low self-esteem to make mistakes, and we modify problems so that they can succeed at each stage towards solving a problem, but we must be wary of taking all the decision-making out of problems.

Managing classroom behaviour

Effective management of classroom behaviour begins at the planning stage. If we are prepared for most of the possible and expected behaviours before we engage with the class, we can have a more balanced and calm view of the proceedings, should they occur.

'A Conjecturing Atmosphere', seen below, is a poster that evolved from children discussing their rights and responsibilities in the classroom – with clear guidance from the teacher. We can plan to help them identify their fears of being wrong, and agree that the kind of classroom we want is one that allows everyone to learn. Used as a classroom poster, we can refer to the agreed principles throughout the year, reminding children that there are reasons why we want to work in this way.

A conjecturing atmosphere . . .

What we want

- An atmosphere where all pupils can learn effectively. This means that we have to learn together.
- A classroom where we can explain our own ideas and others will listen, and build on these ideas.

Why we want it

- Because everyone has the right to learn, and the teacher has the right to teach.
- Mutual respect builds the self-esteem of every individual.
- Because everyone is valued.

How we make it happen

- We talk as a group. We listen as a group. We share what we discover. We cooperate.
- We exchange meaning.
- We listen carefully to explanations and try to understand.
- We test conjectures, e.g. by finding counter-examples, or by helping each other to find a proof.
- We criticise constructively.
- Background noise is kept to a minimum, so that each person is able to think clearly.
- We keep focused on the task.

  - Nobody ridicules.
  - Nobody shouts.
  - Nobody interrupts.

The rules are made to protect the rights and responsibilities of everyone in the classroom, including the teacher. Most behaviour is an aspect of culture –

the vast majority of children will behave in ways they perceive are acceptable within the environment. Very few children will exhibit behaviours that challenge the prevailing culture. So, most misbehaviour is low-level, minor disruption, but if this is left to go unchecked, then more extreme poor behaviour is more likely to occur, as it will emerge more easily from a general atmosphere of disorder.

Routines and expectations are important for establishing order, for example:

- clear expectations of what pupils should do at the beginning of the lesson – whether it is having books and equipment ready, standing quietly behind chairs while waiting to be seated or attempting an activity that is already written on the board;
- a clear signal for wishing to speak, e.g. 'Thank you ladies and gentlemen' usually needs only saying no more than twice; one teacher moves a stool to the front of the classroom and takes a seat to establish calm and silence; another raises a hand to request calm.

Routines and expectations support the requirement of being consistent – both the day-to-day consistency for the individual teacher and across the whole school. Meaning what we say and saying what we mean also reinforce this consistency, always carrying out actions that we say we will take.

Praise is also a valuable tool for establishing calm at the beginning of the lesson: those pupils who respond immediately to your request for silence can be thanked explicitly, even with the use of the school's reward system, and often this will calm a class down very quickly.

These points emphasise that effective management of behaviour stems from the quality of the relationships between teachers and pupils. There are ways in which these professional relationships can be enhanced. Teachers should consider:

- **Body position/language**
  Note carefully that speaking at eye level is less threatening than standing over a pupil.

- **Tone of voice/use of language**
  We must model proper conduct at all times.

- **Keeping calm**
  This is much easier when you have confidence in your own ways of establishing order in the classroom – hence planning for managing behaviour, and if necessary rehearsing your actions in response to behaviours you can predict. Confidence also arises from being sure of the consequences

if poor behaviour should exceed that which is normally tolerated in the classroom.

- **Repair and rebuild**
  If things go wrong, it is important the child recognises that there is no grudge, and that there is a way back to the classroom where learning can take place again. It is best to try to ensure that you and the child can talk, calmly and quietly, away from the classroom, in preparation for the child's return to the next lesson.

If creating this climate for learning enables children to discuss their mathematical ideas freely, we are also allowing ourselves the chance to assess their understanding and to address their misconceptions more effectively.

Collaboration

To extend the opportunities for creating a mutually supportive (and therefore successful) classroom, we must also look at how groups or pairs of pupils can be helped to work collaboratively. There are sound educational reasons for collaborative working and joint problem-solving, and focusing on how children handle the vocabulary of mathematics in their discussions. As Lave and Wenger (1991) point out, there is a difference between 'talking *about* a practice from outside and talking *within* it'.

The example of a lesson described in Chapter 4 and Figure 4.2 illustrates a problem solved by pupils in pairs, where they are making decisions about what percentages of a quantity they wish to find, and learning about how their methods can be refined so that they can find any percentage of any quantity. This requires a rethink in the style of activity:

- open – 'find out whatever percentages you can' – rather than closed – 'complete this set of pre-written questions';
- seating arrangements (for pair work rather than individual work); and
- resources used (e.g. large paper, rather than individual books).

It also requires a change in view about what acceptable outcomes of a lesson look like – rather than a neat page of written work, children discuss solutions effectively or explain their own ideas. Sometimes this means nothing is written. There is no need for the teacher or pupil to feel guilty about that.

Collaborative pair working can also be a useful technique in whole-class discussions: if children have an opportunity to articulate some of their ideas to their partners, they have opportunities to refine their ideas, overcome mistakes and use the vocabulary correctly before addressing the whole class. This is also a valuable point of intervention from other adults working in the class (see Chapter 5 Managing support and intervention).

MacGrath (1998) states that other advantages to facilitating cooperative relationships among pupils include:

- The greater the cooperation among pupils, the less conflict is likely between them.
- In an atmosphere of relative harmony, one potential source of anger that could be directed towards the teacher is eliminated.
- Pupils can help [and] more pupils can succeed and will have a greater investment in making school work for them.

It is important to plan the *purposes* of the collaborations taking place in the class. In classrooms where children can seem highly dependent on the teacher to overcome a range of difficulties (whether it is drawing a diagram, reading a piece of text or explaining the next step), planning for children to help each other can take the pressure off the teacher, and allows children to take responsibility for the success of the class. This point will be developed more fully in the section on differentiation in the next chapter, but as McNamara and Moreton (1997) suggest: 'In our view all children should have the opportunity to be a tutor and in particular teachers should ensure that children with low self-esteem have the opportunity to be a tutor.' This means that the purposes need not just be restricted to facilitating access to learning (reading text for each other, making diagrams), but can be focused on the learning itself, e.g. explaining ideas to each other.

The physical environment and resources for learning

Look at your room and ask yourself some questions, for instance:

- Is the wall display used to enhance learning?
- Is the equipment labelled to help children's independence?
- Does the seating help children to work collaboratively?
- Is furniture arranged so that wheelchair users can move around freely?

The physical environment can help us address some specific principles:

- Children need to be clear about the focus of the lesson – they need to know what they are learning, so that they can identify their own success – so the objectives of the lesson have a space at the front of the class.
- Demonstrations and instructions should be clear – accessible to all, and uncluttered.
- Children should learn to talk and must have a clear view of the vocabulary

relevant to the lesson – therefore this vocabulary needs to be displayed, in such a way that it can be easily accessed.

- Children need opportunities to become independent mathematicians – they need easy access to materials and equipment, which they can then use to model, demonstrate and reason.

Pupils who use a wheelchair or other mobility aid will need a clear route to their desks and sufficient space to turn and manoeuvre in order to collect equipment. Pupils with physical disabilities should be involved in decisions about where they sit in the class. Consideration will also need to be given to the height and position of tables and chairs.

Some children with special educational needs may struggle with too much information, such as cluttered walls and cupboards, or with unclear writing on the board or on displays.

Appendices 4–9 illustrate some ideas for the use of the board and some posters.

The whiteboard, interactive whiteboards, computers and projectors

You need a decent sized board, or one large and one or two small boards either side or on other walls, where the objectives and vocabulary of the lesson can be easily viewed and referred to. If you are lucky enough to have an interactive whiteboard even better, but the overriding principle is that children learn better when they know where they are going (clear objectives) and have the tools (vocabulary) readily displayed. These are ongoing, updated displays and should become a norm for each lesson.

There is debate about whether to use whiteboards because the glare from the many light sources to be found in classrooms can be distracting to pupils. You will have specific information about any visual difficulties your children experience – some may react to bright light, others to low light, and some children may not benefit from enlarging texts or diagrams because their vision is concentrated onto one area. A discussion with your SENCO would clarify any uncertainties. If glare is a concern, you could perhaps consider using different coloured pens, adjusting the classroom lighting or reducing the brightness of the projector.

Often children with communication difficulties will need opportunities to express their understanding physically, and therefore to come out and demonstrate using diagrams or by moving shapes about. This can be done manually (pens, paper, etc.) or by making use of an interactive whiteboard. There are many useful tools built into interactive whiteboard software (such as Promethean

ActivInspire or SMART Notebook) for this, including Cuisenaire rods, scales, thermometer, clocks, graphs, shapes, etc., that are straightforward to manipulate in order to aid demonstration. With an interactive whiteboard, different coloured backgrounds can be easily used, should you teach children who may find reading easier with a different background.

Projectors linked to computers are also excellent sources of display. As with interactive whiteboards, the capacity to save information and the access to dynamic software (in geometry and graphical work especially) mean they are powerful tools for focusing children on the mathematics. Children's attention is enhanced, and the experience of whole-group discussion based on accurate and clear diagrams, charts and graphs reduces scope for misunderstandings.

As with all resources, we must decide if using ICT is the most appropriate medium for learning. The disadvantage of computers linked to projectors lies in the extent to which they inhibit your interaction with the class if you are stuck behind a computer. We should be actively teaching, and if we are, we need to point to things and demonstrate ideas, not just set off a slideshow. Interactive whiteboards enable you to move and emphasise, and children are often keen to use them too in order to demonstrate their ideas and understanding.

The classroom number line (see Appendices 4, 5 and 10)

This is essential. Blank number lines can be used for developing progression in understanding all four operations (see Chapter 3), for comparing fractions, decimals and percentages, generating number sequences, and for the 0–1 scale in probability. As a visual tool for making calculations, it can be referred to regularly. It needs to be large enough to read clearly from any point in the classroom, and also to illustrate counting by large hand movements or walking from one number to the next.

Consider flexibility here also. Although a classroom number line with the numbers from −10 to 10 is shown in Appendix 4 as a way of helping children understand the relative sizes of negative numbers, and operations using negative numbers, it is also worth considering leaving the line blank, ready for any of the uses indicated above, and ready for a range of positions (e.g. from 20 to 40) or scales (e.g. from −100 to 100 or a scale involving decimals).

Vocabulary lists

The more children handle the vocabulary of mathematics, the more they become empowered as mathematicians. Subject-specific wordwalls are becoming increasingly common, but it is useful to review their purpose, and perhaps look at alternative ways of helping children focus on vocabulary.

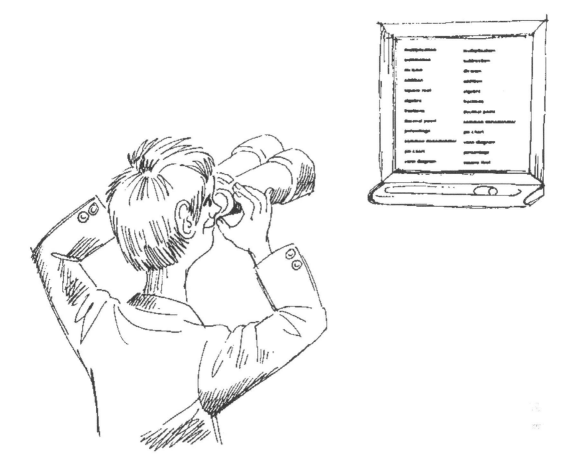

It would be impossible to place the entire glossary of mathematical terms on a wall. Furthermore, long lists of words can become sterile and will be of little use to pupils. Lesson or topic vocabulary lists, placed in an easy point of reference during discussions, however, enable you to focus children's attention on the language, its meanings and spellings (e.g. note discrete/discreet). You can then ask them to use the words to develop the quality of their explanations of their ideas, as you point to the words they could use. The vocabulary lists thus become a more dynamic learning aid.

Pupils' work

This is a way of explicitly valuing children's contributions. It only needs to be a few examples of work that clearly demonstrate what both you and the children feel are good pieces of work. With that in mind, it does not necessarily mean that the work has to look good, but it could give an opportunity for the children to annotate the work with an explanation of what they have found out. This process of explanation deepens their understanding.

Alternative recording methods

These include:

- photographs or videos of pupils engaged in practical tasks;
- photographs of completed work using physical materials, e.g. Cuisenaire rods, card sorts, shapes;
- recordings of pupils' responses (dictaphone apps on smartphones can be used);
- scribing;
- cut-and-stick methods for pupils who have difficulties with written tasks.

Resources/mathematical equipment

Since some children with special educational needs have yet to master objectives usually related to younger children, we sometimes have difficulty in finding resources and equipment that are relevant and meaningful to older age groups. The 'textbook for older children with SEND' does not – and perhaps should not – exist. In any series of lessons written at a distance from the classroom, it is likely that the first one goes reasonably well, but the teacher will identify some issues from questioning the pupils which will prompt responsive planning for the next lesson. The more skilful the teacher in assessing pupils' understanding in the first lesson, the more responsive the second lesson should be, and the third, and so on. You can't write a textbook to do that, and with children with SEND the cycle of plan, teach, learn, assess, evaluate, respond is even more critical to enable them to learn effectively.

An effectively resourced mathematics department will attempt to address the learning of the various mathematical topics (number, algebra, geometry, data handling, ratio and proportion) through a range of teaching and learning styles (see Chapter 3). Appendix 11 offers a list of physical resources for a mathematics department – although it applies equally to an inclusive mathematics classroom. Berger *et al.* (2000) suggest we identify and use 'age neutral resources', and there are many useful resources listed here for effective teaching in mathematics, none of which look like a textbook. The range of resources allows us to develop a greater repertoire of teaching techniques.

Unfortunately, some people seem to believe in a hierarchy of knowledge that operates in a way that makes practical knowledge less valid than 'knowledge in the head'. No one learns to drive a car from reading instructions in a book and getting straight in to operate the clutch and gearshift immediately and brilliantly. Driving a car is a prized *practice*, but so are hypothesising, designing questionnaires and conducting surveys; reasoning, explaining and proving; constructing, modelling and evaluating. Using mathematical equipment allows children to engage in these practices with a visual and tactile stimulus.

For example, interlocking cubes can be used to generate sequences:

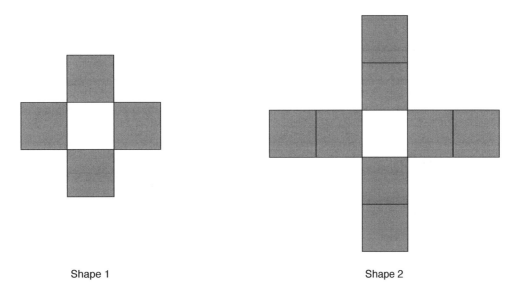

Shape 1   Shape 2

Figure 2.1 Building a sequence of shapes using interlocking cubes

The following instructions and questions develop the lesson:

- *Build the third shape.*
- How many grey cubes?
- How many white cubes?
- How many cubes altogether?
- What about the fourth shape? How do you know?
- The tenth shape? How do you know?
- The hundredth shape? How do you know?
- *Create a table of results* (see Table 2.2 overleaf).
- Is there a pattern in the numbers?
- Is there a way of working out how many there are in the hundredth shape without counting?
- Why do we put the results in order?
- *Extend the table of results to include larger numbers* (see Table 2.2).
- What about the twentieth shape?
- The millionth? How do we write this?
- How does this help us write an expression for the number of cubes in the nth shape?
- Is there always one white cube?

At a million, we know that each arm has one million grey cubes, so there are four million grey cubes + 1 white cube altogether. This can be written as 4m+1 for short here; m for million, eventually moving towards n for any, gets children into the *practice* of representing sequences algebraically . . . for it is a practice, just like driving. Further, children can see the physical development of a sequence and explain why their rule is four times the shape number plus one (because there are four arms and one in the middle). This gives them an opportunity to reason.

Table 2.2 Creating a table of results from a sequence of shapes

Shape number	Number of white cubes	Number of grey cubes	Total number of cubes
1	1	4	5
2	1	8	
3			
4			
5			
10			
20			
m			
n			

The same cubes can be used to build shapes, exploring relationships between volume and surface area, and so on. However, the mathematical equipment is sterile without appropriate questions to stimulate thinking.

For instance, if we build a cuboid with dimensions $2 \times 3 \times 4$, would we need twice as many cubes if we doubled the dimensions?

This is just one example of using equipment to develop mathematical thinking. It is beyond the scope of this book to examine the use of all the equipment listed – but examples of some of the questions are given below.

Cuisenaire rods

Cuisenaire rods can be used to form 'factor walls' or 'fraction walls' (see Figure 2.2 and 2.3 overleaf). Questions could emerge such as: 'How many red rods make the same length as the orange?'

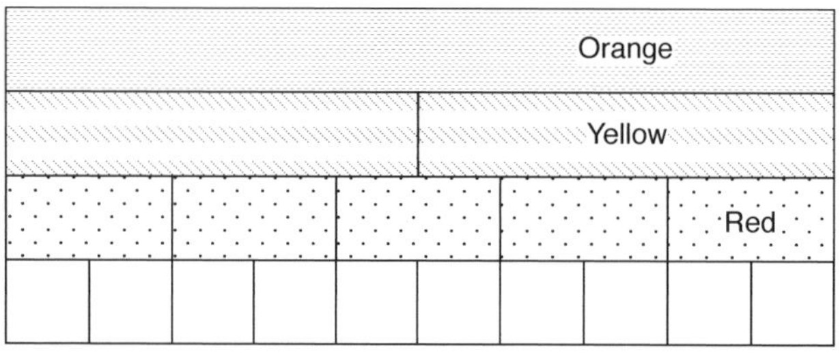

Figure 2.2 Building a Cuisenaire fraction wall

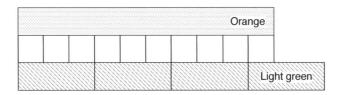

Figure 2.3 Demonstrating that 3 is not a factor of 10

A Cuisenaire factor wall can easily become a fraction wall if we talk about 10 whites = 1 orange rod, so 1 white is $\frac{1}{10}$ of an orange rod, and so on.

Figure 2.3 demonstrates that 3 is not a factor of 10 (the *light green* rods do not fit exactly into the orange) but it is still a *fraction* of ten ($\frac{3}{10}$).

Labelling

It is important to consider labelling all the equipment clearly to enable children to become independent and spontaneous users of it. To demonstrate an idea, we often need to model a situation using equipment. For example, in showing that if 4 + 6 = 10, so 6 + 4 = 10 (demonstrating the commutative law of addition), we could use Cuisenaire rods again (Figure 2.4).

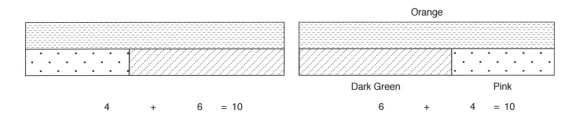

Figure 2.4 Modelling mathematical ideas – the commutative law of addition, illustrated using Cuisenaire rods

Ideally we would want children to learn to demonstrate rules in these ways. Feeling free to use equipment is a small step towards this.

Displays, posters

Appendices 5–9 illustrate possibilities for the classroom walls, if you are lucky enough to have any to work with. It is highly unlikely you will have four walls – one is bound to be a bank of windows but the ideas are there to adapt.

Times table charts (Appendices 7 and 8)

These provide an excellent aid to help understand the relationships between the tables; they can be used as frequent lesson starters to rehearse table skills and explore the links in the number system.

100 squares (Appendix 9)

There are many commercially manufactured 100 squares, with ideas for activities. Consider some 100 squares that start with 1 at the bottom (Appendix 9), to aid the language of 'going up in tens', 'getting larger', etc.

The data handling cycle

The diagram shown in Figure 2.5 is useful in a number of ways:

- To help children identify where they are in solving a problem – so that they know what they might need to do next, or so that they can understand where their current work fits into the whole picture. So, for example, if children have collected their data, they can be guided towards processing (making calculations) or representing their data (choosing the right charts, graphs or diagrams).
- To help children evaluate how they are working. For example, if children have interpreted data but find that their conclusions cannot say anything about their original hypothesis, they need to go back to their original plans and address how they designed their questionnaires, or review the decision they made on what data to collect.
- The cycle illustrates to teachers that each phase has a place in the overall context, e.g. teaching children *about* graphs and bar charts, by giving them lots of practice in drawing them for different situations, is not the same as teaching children how to use them, and why, and these aspects must be explicitly taught.

- As a planning tool, teachers can identify which parts of the cycle children need to practise further. If children are weak in interpreting their results, this might highlight a need for plenty of discussion based on a range of graphs, charts and diagrams.

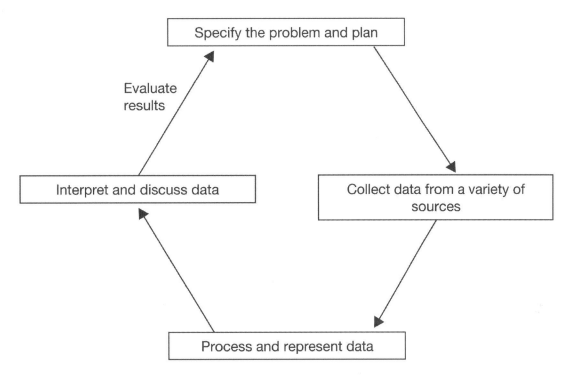

Figure 2.5 The data handling cycle

Mathematical papers

The wide variety of mathematical papers provides a range of opportunities for different mathematical activities. Some very large centimetre squared paper is useful, especially for drawing fractions of a number line, where the line is 60 cm long. This is a good number because it has many factors, and many fractions of it can be found. Other papers bring in other mathematical ideas – isometric dotty is useful for translating 3D images onto 2D paper, and children can count the dots to help them draw shapes with the correct dimensions. Appendix 13 shows examples of some activities based on different types of dotty paper (see also Appendices 14–16).

Wider considerations in planning

Many teachers are concerned that maths lessons have to reflect and develop other areas of learning such as literacy. Effective planning should ensure that this becomes an integral part of maths lessons. There is no additional planning for literacy, because we are planning for 'mathematical literacy' in the ways we promote handling vocabulary, and children discussing, reasoning, explaining, etc. Our writing has a specific mathematical purpose.

For some children with SEND, a writing frame provides an effective structure to their thinking. Appendix 17 offers a possible example for structuring a data handling project. Work in data handling has much to do with convincing others of interpretations of data. This can be expressed orally or in writing, and then presented to the whole group. Formal presentations of findings from statistical surveys can lead to children justifying their results, and the class engaging in joint evaluation of the findings.

Again, this relies on a conjecturing atmosphere, where it is safe for pupils to have their work analysed publicly, but their literacy skills are developed in an activity that has authenticity and, therefore, credibility. Mathematical literacy is not developed through word searches, but through this kind of meaningful activity.

We could use a similar example to illustrate how we are developing children's experience of citizenship. We become citizens through experiencing our society's practices and reflecting on these experiences. In the example given above, a classroom is described that can be likened to a community of young mathematicians, who may generate hypotheses, identify the information they require to convince others that their hypotheses are correct (or not), present this information in ways to illustrate their arguments, and then justify their results and methods. Other pupils can then explain why they are convinced (or not) and try to formulate appropriate questions. This is one example of modelling how we can operate as effective citizens. Planning these lessons takes into account how the class will collaborate, as well as the mathematics the children will learn.

Inclusive classrooms therefore address the entitlement of all pupils to all aspects of learning, and each of these aspects is seen as an integral part of the activities of the classroom. Later chapters will look at how to plan for differentiation, assessment and other colleagues in the classroom.

Planning for misconceptions

Even before we teach, it is worth evaluating the planning by at least asking the questions:

- What difficulties will the children have with understanding this (or these) objective(s)?
- How can I prepare to meet these difficulties?

Then you can look at the range of resources (see Appendix 11), ideas, equipment, staffing and collaboration with other pupils as possible solutions to the problems – and you can see the need to plan to use these solutions.

Some examples of lesson objectives are considered below.

Objective: Recognise vertically opposite angles

Possible difficulties – Children may think that the angles have to stand vertically, instead of realising that the angles are vertically opposite however the diagram is rotated; children may not understand which angles are 'opposite'.

Possible solutions – Use colours, as well as conventional notation to indicate the angles that are vertically opposite; use an interactive whiteboard demonstration of two crossing lines – rotate it and clarify that the angles are still vertically opposite. Check their understanding of 'opposite' with simple activities in the classroom.

Objective: Recognise the first few triangular numbers, squares of numbers to at least 12 × 12 and the corresponding roots

Possible difficulties – Children may not relate the term 'square numbers' to the shape of a square, and therefore have no idea that the root of the square's area is equivalent to the length of its side; they may not know how to generate the square or triangular numbers.

Possible solutions – Children make some squares with interlocking cubes or diagrams, find a connection between sides and areas; using squared paper, what different sized squares can they make? What are the areas of these squares? Generate triangular numbers from realistic situations, e.g. How many red snooker balls are there on a normal sized snooker table? What if the table were smaller, and we had to use a smaller triangle? Larger? Explore with triangular diagrams.

Objective: Explain and justify methods and conclusions

Possible difficulties – Children may not be happy to do this in front of the class; they may not remember or know the correct vocabulary to use.

Possible solutions – Refer to vocabulary list; listen to children's explanations, helping them to clarify any points of misunderstanding; emphasise correct use of vocabulary – children may feel happier to address the whole class after speaking to someone one-to-one; child may wish to use an interactive whiteboard for presentation, or get help from a partner who does the presentation with the child's prompting.

A further example of support could be in the use of a speaking/writing prompt, where the language of the problem can be used as a guide. For example, if children were trying to address the topic 'Pupils make simple estimates' (level P8), they might be asked to estimate how many adults would be able to sit on a bench seat (e.g. in a park or at a picnic table). The following lines could be used as a prompt to guide their thinking:

- I think the answer is more than one because . . .
- In half the bench we would be able to fit in . . . adults.
- So in the whole bench we could fit in twice as many, which would make . . .

For larger numbers, different situations could be used, e.g. estimating the number of buttons needed for a shirt:

- The places we need buttons are . . .
- For these places we would need . . . buttons.
- Down the front we would need about . . . buttons to (a specified point, e.g. halfway).
- The total of these buttons is . . .

Through clarifying the language children use, we can clarify their thinking. The writing frame offered in Appendix 17 is another example of this.

Summary

In planning an inclusive classroom, we must start with the question 'How do I empower all pupils to learn?' Through this question we can analyse the physical environment and the resources we use, the nature of the activities we plan for our lessons, the ways in which children work and the nature of the 'conversations they are a part of'.

The following chapters will examine how this looks in practice as we teach, and then how we assess both the children's understanding and our lessons' effectiveness.

3 Teaching and learning

Lesson structure and design

The design of our lessons reflects our beliefs about how children learn. If we believe that children doing pages of sums is an effective way of teaching children an understanding of mathematics, then our lessons would look like that most of the time. If we believe that there is far more than that to effective learning, we may prefer to see lessons where children can articulate their own understanding through guided use of mathematical vocabulary, either orally or through the drafting process in writing; where they experience mathematics through a variety of learning media, including physical activities and resources, visual imagery and ICT; and where they are clear about the goals of their learning. Lessons reflecting the latter views will be designed with variety, based on a series of episodes, and will form part of a clearly planned scheme.

Structured mathematics lessons

Episodic lessons need not be the same as the more traditional three-part lesson (mental and oral starter/main activity/plenary, as suggested in the KS3 National Strategy: *Framework for Teaching Mathematics – Years 7, 8 and 9*, page 28, DfES 2001). However, it should be noted that the three-part lesson plan is an example of episodic teaching, and one should feel free to use this when appropriate. By generalising the idea of episodic teaching we have a greater flexibility to adapt our teaching to the class in front of us. One advantage of episodic teaching is that it allows the teacher to include regular pauses in lessons for reflection/metacognition, often referred to as mini-plenaries. However, the most important point is that an episodic, structured lesson offers us opportunities to use a variety of teaching styles, resources and ideas in order to support the different ways in which children learn.

Starters/check in activities

If being utilised, these offer opportunities for the teacher to:

- develop students' oral/mental mathematics skills;
- check prerequisite skills for that lesson;
- 'warm up' with some piece of written work;
- allow students to connect their work to real-life situations;
- allow students an opportunity to give feedback to the teacher.

None of these aspects should be considered as exclusively the domain of the starter – they can be used as and when appropriate.

The example given later in the section on 'Questioning' illustrates the value of children explaining their own calculation strategies. We could also add to this list:

- the class sharing in joint problem-solving activities – because this may set the tone for the classroom culture we would wish to establish;
- dealing with misconceptions, to iron out some of the likely problems before children engage with a main activity.

Main activities and plenary sessions

Whereas the starter of the lesson could stand in isolation (because it could usefully provide practice in previously learned skills, or address an aspect of mathematics tackled some time ago or to be reviewed in the future), the main teaching and the plenary episodes are more tightly linked. Indeed, it can be argued that plenary sessions are more successful when they emerge meaningfully from the activity that has been going on previously. For example, the activity (Chapter 2) involving the grey and white cubes/squares leads naturally to a question and answer session where the generalisations can be explored, even using symbols to represent the rules that we find. An extended plenary might explore different shapes, e.g.:

Shape 1, using triangles

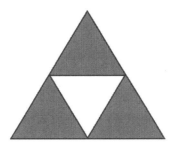

Can you make the next two shapes?

Create a table of results.

Shape number	White triangles	Grey triangles	Total number of triangles
1	1	3	4
2	1		
3			

How does using triangles change the sequence of numbers, from using squares?

Figure 3.1 Developing a sequence of numbers from triangular shapes

The plenary needs careful planning. It offers opportunities to draw together the learning from the lesson; allows pupils to reflect on their progress; allows teachers to assess children's learning, and prepares both teacher and pupils for the following lesson. It is not effective just as a 'going through the answers' session, where no questioning about children's methods takes place – but the plenary offers an opportunity to use questioning effectively to assess understanding in different ways, e.g.:

- **using the rule**, e.g. 'Can you work out the number of cubes for the 100th shape?'
- **understanding how we solve the problem**, e.g. 'What patterns do you notice?' and 'Why do we put the numbers in a table?'
- **applying the rule**, e.g. 'If the total number of cubes used were 61, which shape have we made?'

Objective-led teaching

Setting clear objectives (and identifying learning outcomes) for your learners is an act of empowerment – it enables the pupils to know what is expected of them, and helps them to evaluate their own progress, which in turn develops their own capacity for independence. Black (1999) also highlights the importance of making explicit the goals of assessment, which will be explored more fully in the next chapter.

A difficulty to overcome is finding meaningful, mathematical learning activities that actually meet the objectives. To exemplify this, consider the objective:

> *Know and use the order of operations, including brackets.*

This objective could be met in several ways, but it is worth examining the effectiveness of the various methods:

Method 1

State the rule: BODMAS/BIDMAS/(Brackets/Of, Indices/Divide/Multiply/Add/Subtract) and offer children a range of questions thus:

1   a) $4 + 8 - 2 =$ b) $3 + 2 \times 5 =$ c) $8 + 6 \times 2 =$

These questions are only related in terms of their level of difficulty, rather than being related in terms of enabling children to see trends or patterns in the results (as in Method 2).

Progression in this view of learning is therefore seen by introducing more complexity, e.g.:

2   a) $6(3 + 4) =$ b) $2(1 + 9) =$ c) $3(5 - 2) =$

Further questions could examine the presentation of division within a series of calculations, e.g.:

3   a) $\dfrac{16 + 2}{3}$ b) $\dfrac{8 + 4}{4}$

Figure 3.2 Addressing an objective through a method focused on the acquisition of skills

Such a structure of progression focuses on acquisition of the various small skills – handling division, using brackets, etc. These skills are incorporated into the next activity, but it has an added dimension of enabling pupils to examine the purposes of the order of operations.

Method 2

We could offer children connected sequences of calculations and invite them to identify rules and patterns in the results, e.g.:

Operations using brackets.
Multiplication and division.

Multiplication

1 a) $(2 \times 5) \times 3 =$ b) $2 \times (5 \times 3) =$

2 a) $(3 \times 5) \times 4 =$ b) $3 \times (5 \times 4) =$

3 a) $(4 \times 3) \times 3 =$ b) $4 \times (3 \times 3) =$

4 a) $(3 \times 5) \times 5 =$ b) $3(5 \times 5) =$

5 a) $(10 \times 3) \times 4 =$ b) $10(3 \times 4) =$

6 a) $(1 \times 2) \times 3 =$ b) $1(2 \times 3) =$

7 Write down what you notice with these multiplications. Why do you think this happens?

8 What are the volumes of these cuboids (all measurements are in cms)?

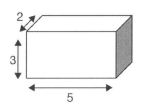 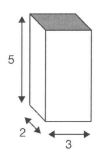

Division

1 a) $(12 \div 6) \div 2 =$ b) $12 \div (6 \div 2) =$

2 a) $(40 \div 10) \div 2 =$ b) $40 \div (10 \div 2) =$

3 a) $(36 \div 6) \div 3 =$ b) $36 \div (6 \div 3) =$

4 a) $(100 \div 10) \div 5 =$ b) $100 \div (10 \div 5) =$

5 a) $(24 \div 6) \div 2 =$ b) $24 \div (6 \div 2) =$

6 a) $(16 \div 2) \div 2 =$ b) $16 \div (2 \div 2) =$

7 Write down what you notice with the answers to these.

8 When do you need to use brackets?

Figure 3.3 Addressing the objective through a method that combines skills acquisition and an understanding of the purpose of the order of the operations

Children could similarly explore addition and subtraction, and also examine the effect of mixed operations. Note this method uses the opportunity to link to another aspect of mathematics – volume of cuboids – to enhance understanding of both the order of operations and the calculation of volumes.

Method 3

We could gather some calculators together (that we know work in different ways, so will produce different answers) and attempt calculations with mixed operations and no brackets, and compare results. This should lead to a discussion about how we can achieve consistency with the results from all calculators, showing the need for brackets, and the need for a convention in the order of operations. Perhaps some of the calculations offered in Methods 1 and 2 above could be used for this.

Figure 3.4 Addressing the objective through a problem to solve

All these methods address the given objective (*Know and use the order of operations, including brackets*):

- **Method 1**
  Could be argued as a direct (and possibly exclusive) teaching of the given objective. Although it may be argued that children are getting practice in calculations with the four operations, this is true of all the methods.

- **Method 2**
  The issue is now placed within a problem-solving context, and further objectives are considered, e.g. *Present and interpret solutions in the context of the original problem; explain and justify (methods and) conclusions, orally and in writing. Use units of measurement to calculate and solve problems involving volume.*

- **Method 3**
  This method could introduce an objective in addition to Method 2, such as: *Carry out calculations with more than one step using brackets and the [calculator's] memory.*

In these methods, a greater range of mathematics emerges when we set the learning within the context of a problem for the class to solve. The second and third methods illustrate *why* we have an order of operations, whereas the first simply presents the rule as a convention for children to take on board. Some may argue that children must learn the skills before they can solve problems with them. However, given that the child who has difficulties with mathematics is likely to take longer on many activities, there is a danger that the wider understanding shown in methods 2 and 3 will be squeezed out if children experience activities where the goal of learning is only the acquisition of skills. It is therefore more likely that this child will experience a disjointed series of skills lessons, without sufficient exploration of their purpose – yet problem-solving is a fundamental aspect of the child's learning.

Teaching to a single objective is therefore not in itself a sufficient guarantee of a high-quality lesson – attention must be paid to a range of objectives, some of which entail problem-solving.

Collaboration and differentiation

Problem-oriented activities emphasise not only agency (the capacity to initiate, explore, complete and evaluate activities, Bruner 1996) but also collaboration. Rogoff (1998), discussing Vygotsky's theory (see Vygotsky 1962), argues that 'the model of most effective social interaction is joint problem-solving with guidance by a person who is more skilled'. In many classrooms, the nature of discussion is often one of children 'reporting' their findings from an activity, and less of children solving problems together through talk. In order to learn *to* talk, rather than *from* talk (Lave and Wenger 1991), we must provide occasions where the real stuff matters so much that students engage in literacy 'as a part of conducting their everyday work in classrooms' (Greeno *et al.* 1997).

The examples given above of setting the mathematics within a problem-solving context enable the teacher to construct paired or group work so that children's findings can be discussed, and their reasoning shared.

McNamara and Moreton (1997) describe a 'model for differentiation', where talk and collaboration are the key features. They state that the rationale for collaboration is that it helps learners to:

- develop their own thinking through talk – by handling the vocabulary through which they think and reason (Bruner 1996);
- get support – to get help in their thought and language development and the emotional support which helps their sense of self-worth and self-belief;
- value their achievements – through collaboration children can be helped to ascribe specific roles and therefore feel a clear sense of responsibility when they are successful in their task.

In pairing or grouping children, this model cites Vygotsky's (1962) view that 'through explaining both partners in the pairing come to realise what it is they are thinking, clarify their thinking and understanding and sometimes come to new thoughts or concepts'.

Meeting differentiation through collaborative pairings addresses differences in learning styles, rather than considering differences in ability. So, for instance, if a child learns best through expressing ideas visually, they may be paired with another who reads and discusses ideas well, and together they can solve a geometric problem that is presented only in written form. Each person has a role to play in the partnership. Collaborative pairings can make meaning through any media – talk, diagrams, physical movements or using a range of mathematical resources for demonstration, but the planning required for this must also focus on the purposes of the collaboration (Murphy 1998).

McNamara and Moreton (1997) go on to argue that for paired activities there are two principles that should be taken into account:

- A joint product should result.
- Collaboration is a criterion for success.

Translating these principles to an activity, we could again refer to the three methods given above for understanding the order of operations. Children could, for instance, be grouped so that they explore the calculator problem (Method 3) together. The joint product could be a report to the class on the effect of changing the order of the terms when using a calculator – for instance, comparing:

a) $2 \times 4 + 5 =$ with b) $5 + 4 \times 2 =$

Part of their joint product could be to find other examples to explore and to check each other's calculations and to calculate using pencil and paper, as well as reporting on the effects for different calculators.

To illustrate how collaboration was a key for success, they could also report on the various roles taken by members of the group, how they supported each other when they came across difficulties, and how successful they were at completing the work. This could be a time-budgeted part of the lesson.

There are too many benefits from this way of working for it to be ignored:

- it will evolve a mutually supportive classroom culture;
- children can work on their own targets with immediate support;
- responsibility for learning is firmly located with the child (teachers are responsible for the *management* of learning);
- problem-oriented activities can be used as the basis of the lesson.

It is also an expression of inclusion through valuing diversity, by using different learning styles in collaboration, and this clearly benefits learning.

Differentiation should also be addressed through effective, focused and planned questioning. Bloom's (1956) taxonomy is a useful tool to help plan questions that require different levels of thinking. This is explored more fully in the next section.

Questioning

The quality of questioning is a key feature of effective mathematics teaching. This can be analysed in a number of ways (e.g. by examining the questions themselves through constructs such as Bloom's taxonomy, or by considering open and closed questioning, or by examining their social impact, such as when to question, and how to manage it in class).

Both the quality of questioning and the impact of teachers' responses can be analysed through the following example:

Teacher: 'Eight sevens?'

Pupil A, holding out 10 digits, says quietly to himself '70', then with 9 digits '63', then with 8 digits he says '56' out loud.

Not all pupils are paying attention.

Teacher – to next pupil: 'Eight sixes?'

Next pupil (B) is completely stuck.

The questions being asked of this class are closed, and the impression is that each pupil has to devise some quick way of answering without learning explicitly from each other. It is worth considering what kind of classroom culture would exist with this group in two years' time. Berger *et al.* (2000) emphasise the importance of giving children time to respond. A feature of many mathematics classrooms is the perceived norm of an automatic response to questions. The correct answer should not always be the aim of questioning – the working out and forming an explanation are more important goals, and these processes take time.

These waiting moments can also be used to praise a class for waiting, for not butting in, and teachers can model the patience and reinforce the values that we are in a learning environment, and that we support people by allowing space and time to each other, not by giving the answers. This helps to build a mutually supportive and, therefore, successful classroom. Shouting out the answers stops children from undertaking the necessary thinking to get to the answer.

What learning could take place if the following happened instead?

Teacher: 'Eight sevens?'

Pupil A, holding out 10 digits, says quietly to himself '70', then with 9 digits '63', then with 8 digits he says '56' out loud.

Teacher: 'I like what you are doing here' (using praise). 'You're using a system' (explaining why the praise was due) – 'how did you work that out?'

Pupil: 'I know that ten sevens are 70, so I counted two sevens back.'

Teacher to class: 'Why did he count two sevens back?' (and tries to model responses on the board . . .)

Pupil: 'He had ten sevens, but you asked for eight sevens, so you have to take two sevens away.'

Figure 3.5 models the pupil's calculation diagrammatically – building a visual image for the pupils. The number line is a powerful tool for this.

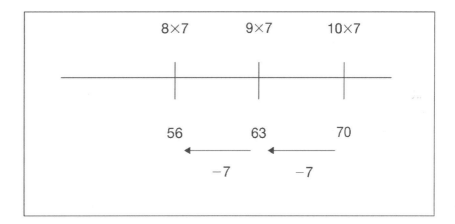

Figure 3.5 Modelling a child's explanation, using a number line

Now, turning to pupil B who claimed to be stuck, the response could be:

Teacher: 'How could we use this method to calculate eight sixes?'

Pupil B might still claim to be stuck, but now there is some scaffolding on the board for understanding how the problem could be tackled.

Teacher: 'Could we use this work on the board to help us find the answer?'

(Continued)

There are several ways to use it, e.g.:

- repeat the model for 10 × 6, then 9 × 6 and then 8 × 6;
- extend the above diagram to count back to 8 × 6.

Or use other methods from other children, e.g.:

- 2 × 6, doubled and doubled again
- 8 × 3, doubled.

Through comparison of children's methods, we are not only helping with the skills of multiplying, but also giving greater insights into the workings of the number system, and showing that we value their methods by explicitly using them in other problems.

The kind of classroom culture that is being developed here is a genuine valuing of pupils' methods, thus building their self-esteem, but we are also evaluating a range of possible methods, finding which are effective and which could not always be applied, suggesting that that is what we do in mathematics classrooms. And we are not saying that pupils are on their own in their learning – solving 8 × 6 could become a class problem to solve.

Such questioning also offers a greater number of opportunities to praise children, and as Hart (2000) states: 'A heightened sense of acknowledgement might be what persuades pupils to take whatever enhanced learning opportunities are introduced.' Praise is essential in building self-esteem and a positive classroom culture, and we can construct opportunities to use it meaningfully through our questioning – and this is a small but practical example of 'valuing diversity and difference' which underpins inclusion.

It is worth considering again what kind of classroom culture would exist in two years' time in a class where these kinds of interactions regularly took place.

Berger *et al.* (2000) offer this classification of questions:

- recalling facts;
- applying facts;
- hypothesising and predicting;
- designing and comparing procedures;
- interpreting;
- applying reasoning.

Children only experience 'recalling facts' when presented with a times table question, but the question 'How did you work that out?' immediately offers children the chance to design and compare procedures, and when this line of questioning is explored, they can go on to use reasoning and apply facts. Effective differentiation is therefore achieved through this type of questioning as it is specific and focused on the point of learning for each child. One question ('How did you work that out?') is relevant to the child who is able to use a method but may need to explain it to be sure of it, whereas another question ('How could we use this method for an alternative problem?') requires the next child to recognise the applicability of a method they may not have considered before.

Using this classification, we can also analyse some written questions and illuminate how different styles of questions allow children scope for wider learning opportunities. A classic GCSE Foundation paper question is given below.

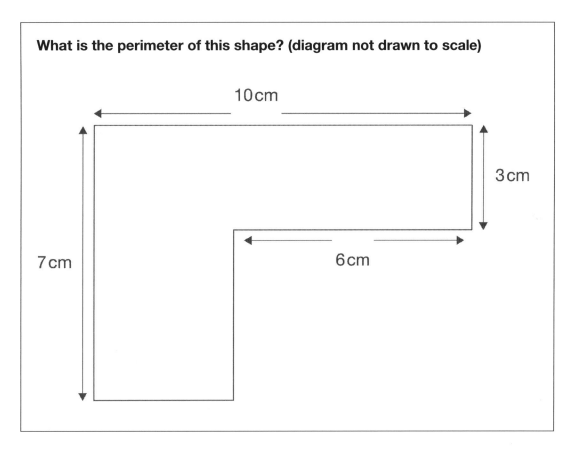

Figure 3.6a GCSE style question on finding the perimeter of a shape

Returning to the question at the beginning of Chapter 2 – 'What do we learn in mathematics lessons?' – we can examine what children learn from answering this question. Here, children are expected to interpret the problem and realise that they need further information – the remaining two lengths – so that they can add up six lengths to find the perimeter. Usually, if children do not understand the method, we can support them but, given this closed example, we are in danger of doing the whole thing for them. Nevertheless, the question invites children to apply reasoning to find the perimeter. However, as Prestage and Perks (2001) suggest, changing the question will change the mathematics that children experience. What happens when we remove some of the information?

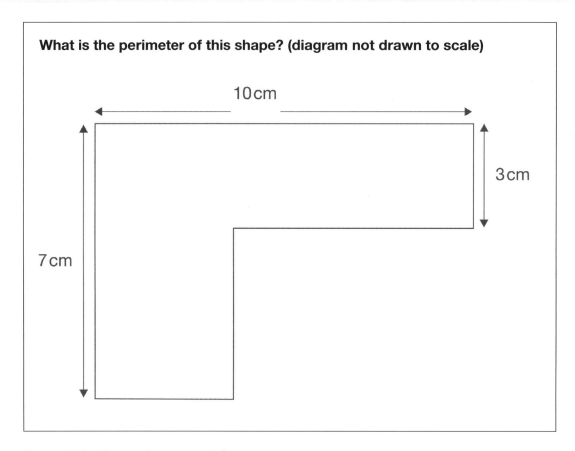

Figure 3.6b Removing some information

Here, children may be encouraged to ask 'What if . . .?', such as 'What if the missing length were 8 cm or 5 cm, etc., and practise the style of the question. However, if they collected all their results and were encouraged to say what they noticed, they might find that all the perimeters were the same. These simple techniques take children who have difficulties with their mathematics into discussing, reasoning, hypothesising and predicting (using Berger *et al.*'s classification), enabling them to make real sense of the mathematics they are encountering.

Finally, if we presented the problem with just the 7 cm and the 10 cm sides given, could the children still work out the perimeter? How do they work it out?

The mathematics takes another level of thinking, because it is now focused on the *concept* of perimeter rather than on the *calculation* of it. This is a far deeper understanding than is enabled through the first question.

Changing the presentation of questions

Some basic sums could be presented thus:

$$
\begin{array}{cccc}
43 & 82 & 98 & 54 \\
+\ \underline{28} & +\ \underline{49} & +\ \underline{14} & +\ \underline{57}
\end{array}
$$

Figure 3.7 Standard presentation of sums

The purpose of these is simply to practise a particular algorithm, namely to use column addition techniques, involving carrying tens (or hundreds). These sums do not necessarily help children understand the *concept* of addition, but they enable them to practise the *written technique* for solving them. If children do not understand what these presentations of addition mean, they need to look at number lines or physical objects (e.g. money, metre sticks, Diene's blocks or other place value tools) to help. They may also need to use these tools to help with the calculation.

Another issue with this presentation of the calculation is that it immediately guides children into one way of solving the problem – through the standard written algorithm. That's fine if that is the objective – but many of our children with SEND need to build their own mental strategies for calculating well before they engage with the written form.

If the first sum were presented horizontally, e.g. 43 + 28, what other strategies might we encourage? There are a few:

- the use of the number line (discussed in the section later in this chapter on visual imagery);
- the use of partitioning: 43 + 28 = (40 + 20) + (3 + 8) = 60 + 11 = 71
- compensation: 43 + 28 = 41 + 30 (by moving two from 43 to the 28) = 71.

Alternatively, if the sum were presented in a more open way, we could encourage children to look for patterns. (A detailed look at the use of patterns is given later in this chapter.) By blotting out the 40, for example, we can have 10 sums.

3 + 28 =

3 + 28; 13 + 28; and so on.

Here, we can encourage children to find what is the same, and what changes in each answer. This will give children an opportunity to learn a self-checking mechanism – that every time an 8 and 3 are added in the units, a one will result in the units column. The use of pattern is a powerful tool in checking accuracy.

It will also give a greater insight into place value, by analysing the effect of changing the value in the tens column.

Children who experience difficulties in mathematics need to have these points made explicit, to clarify their understanding. To do this, children must discuss their own findings and ideas – to create their own understanding 'instead of rehearsing or recreating knowledge produced by others' (Wiske 1998).

Appendix 18 looks at some mathematical questioning through Bloom's taxonomy. However, this taxonomy should not be considered as a hierarchy of increasing exclusivity. For instance, all children could have the chance to:

- look at poorly drawn graphs and say what might be wrong with them (Appendix 19);
- predict later numbers in a sequence;
- analyse results from a statistical survey.

All pupils are entitled to deal with the higher levels of questioning that this taxonomy helps us to identify.

Adapting teaching to maximise progress (including learning styles)

A teacher for the inclusive classroom must recognise that restricting learning opportunities to one favoured style of presenting ideas – presentations both by the teacher and by the children – will disadvantage some pupils in the class. The development of research in learning styles has raised our awareness of the need to consider a range of learning activities not just for the sake of children's access and expression but also because it is clear that the mathematical content – and thus what can be learned from the activities – takes on different qualities when using different media.

Take, for example, a problem from Ollerton (2003, page 16 – 'Wholesome triangles'):

1. How many different triangles can be made with a perimeter of 30 cm so that all sides are of whole number length?

This can be presented to children in a number of ways.

Restricting children to writing down their answers as numbers may mean that they fall into the trap of thinking they are only looking for sets of three whole numbers that sum to 30, e.g. 1, 1, 28; 1, 2, 27; 2, 2, 26, etc., without realising that these initial solutions could not possibly make a triangle. They have therefore interpreted the problem as a 'sum to 30' exercise, instead of a 'three possible sides of a triangle' problem (see Figure 3.8).

Even with the aid of diagrams, some children may still fall into this trap, because there is no 'real' or physical experience underpinning their presentation of results.

For some children, it is only when using sticks or string cut to appropriate whole-number lengths that they will recognise *both* conditions of the problem – that the perimeter is 30 cm *and* that the three sides have to fit together to form a triangle.

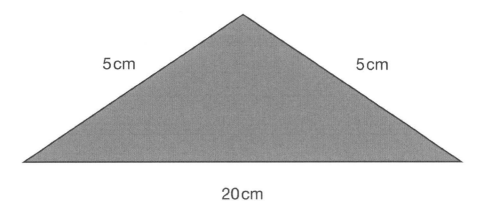

Figure 3.8 A 'problem' triangle!

This should be viewed as a learning activity, not an assessment task, but even then we should ask why an assessment task should be restricted to the written number form. As a learning activity, children are provided with a greater insight into the relationship between the sides of a triangle when they have something physical to manipulate.

For some people, using physical resources represents a lower order of mathematical understanding, for use only with younger children and those who experience difficulties. For others, there may be concerns that presenting ideas physically or using diagrams slows down the pace of lessons, and that there is enough pressure to 'cover' the curriculum as it is.

If our first principle is to create an inclusive classroom, then we must be concerned about building the self-esteem of pupils, and we must ensure that we meet their rights to understand the ideas we are teaching, and we therefore use the range of techniques necessary to achieve this. Children are entitled to the self-esteem that arises from understanding/mastery, and any means to achieve that should be explored.

Some of the ways we could vary the learning styles in the mathematics classroom are illustrated in Table 3.1.

Table 3.1 Examples of ways to vary learning styles

Learning style	Support learning through
Visual	Wall displays, posters, flash cards, graphic organisers, graphs, charts, number lines, spider diagrams, videos, concept maps, colour highlighting (e.g. colour angles which are the same in diagrams).
Auditory	Use MP3s, videos, storytelling, chants and visualisations.
	Allow learners to work in pairs and small groups regularly.
	Discussion, stories. Collaborative writing – presentations for the class. Talking about the vocabulary, e.g. explaining the term 'percentage' and its roots in 'cent – 100' and other real-life uses of the root 'cent' – century.
Kinaesthetic	Use physical activities, competitions, board games, role-plays, whiteboards, movement (e.g. illustrating that angle is a measurement of turn, experiencing rotations), card-sorting. Use a range of mathematical equipment, e.g. interlocking cubes, rods, geometrical strips, Taktiles (*Algebra through Geometry* pack – G. Giles), probability experiments.
	Intersperse activities that require students to sit quietly with activities that allow them to move around and be active.

It is worth exploring, in a little detail, how some of the techniques for teaching with different learning styles can enhance understanding in different ways. Some schools/teachers have considered the idea of preferred learning styles (i.e. identifying which way particular students learn best) but, given the desire for an inclusive classroom, a blend is usually sufficient. Remember a student favouring one learning style does not exclude them from accessing learning via other methods.

Visual imagery

The number line (Appendices 4, 5 and 10) was introduced in Chapter 2. It is worth briefly demonstrating its power, both as a visual aid and as a way of identifying progression in learning calculating techniques with all four operations – addition, subtraction, multiplication and division.

Firstly, the blank number line may be presented in different forms, depending on the level of support you wish to offer the child.

Some examples of how these lines may be used with all four number operations are illustrated overleaf.

Marked and labelled

Marked and unlabelled

Empty number line

_____

Focusing on different sections of the number line

Figure 3.9 Different types of number line

Addition

Addition can be seen as *counting on*, using each integer as a step, or by using larger jumps, say in fives or tens, when children become more comfortable with counting in this way. The steps can be used to illustrate the mental processes that children employ, for example:

4 + 12 = 16

Children may calculate this as 4 + 2 + 10 (Figure 3.10a) or 4 + 10 + 2 (Figure 3.10b) or 4 + 6 + 6 = 10 + 6 = 16 (Figure 3.10c).

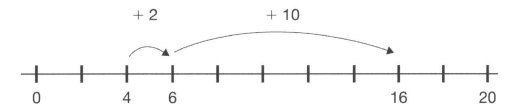

Figure 3.10a 4 + 12 = 4 + 2 + 10 = 16

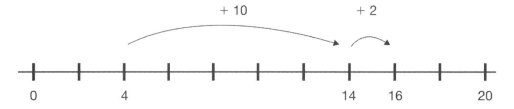

Figure 3.10b 4 + 12 = 4 + 10 + 2 = 16

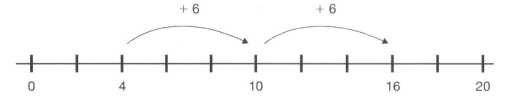

Figure 3.10c 4 + 12 = 4 + 6 + 6 = 10 + 6 = 16

Illustrating children's different methods visually allows others to compare their own methods, and offers different insights into the number system. Using the last example highlights the value of complements to ten as a mental addition technique; the first two show that, when adding ten, the unit value does not change.

The technique can be extended to handling decimals, and indeed this reinforces the understanding of the patterns and similarities throughout the number system, e.g.:

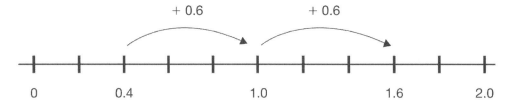

Figure 3.10d 0.4 + 1.2 = 0.4 + 0.6 + 0.6 = 1.0 + 0.6 = 1.6

Subtraction

Subtraction using the number line builds on these ideas of using counting on. It's a bit like a visual form of giving change by counting to useful whole numbers of tens or hundreds.

Teaching children about the 'mechanics' of subtraction has long been separated from establishing an understanding of subtraction. By setting out subtraction calculations in columns, and devising ingenious methods for dealing with 'borrowing' or 'paying back', we fail to address an understanding of difference. In contrast, looking at the calculation using a number line, or working out how much change to give, involves communication and checking which aids under-standing. Teaching children the column method does not help them understand the *concept* of differences or of subtraction; it teaches only about the method. Further, there is little scope for progression in teaching column subtraction, because it has to be significantly modified in the type of situation given below. When the method goes wrong, however, the children have little recourse to understanding why, and do not – or cannot – check their work.

For example:

$$
\begin{array}{r}
105 \\
-68 \\
\hline
163
\end{array}
$$

Figure 3.11 A common subtraction error

The answer is meaningless, but this happens often because children are using a method they do not understand, to work on a concept they do not under-stand. In this case, the child has taken the 5 from the 8, and the zero tens from the 60. It's much easier to deal with than taking the 8 from the 5, and the 60 from zero.

If we taught for understanding through progression and by developing visual imagery through the number line, children would have a chance of seeing whether their answers made sense or not. This would not cure everything, but it would give children a way of 'seeing' the subtraction, and help to give them a feel for the validity of their answers. It relies on children knowing complements to ten (and multiples of ten), complements to 100 (in tens), and then adding two single digit numbers to a multiple of ten.

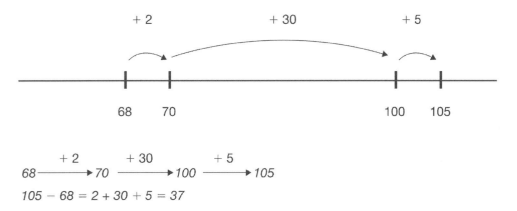

$105 - 68 = 2 + 30 + 5 = 37$

Figure 3.12 105 – 68 using the number line

This technique can be used for any subtraction calculation, and thus genuinely builds progression.

Multiplication and division

Although division can be seen as repeated subtraction, and the standard written method of long division reinforces this link, many children also use the links between multiplication and division to help them solve problems. Using the number line again, these links can be clearly illustrated.

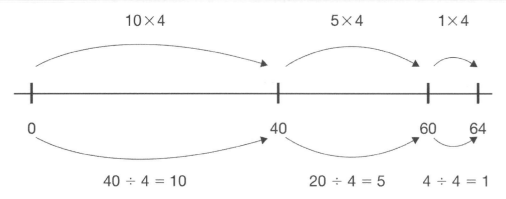

Figure 3.13 Showing the links between multiplication (16 × 4 = 64) and division (64 ÷ 4 = 16)

All division and multiplication calculations – through to large numbers and decimals/fractions – can be represented in this way as a means of scaffolding children's understanding.

Other skills and understanding come into play:

- using known multiplication bonds, e.g. 10 × 4 = 40, 5 × 4 = 20, to bridge towards the product or dividend;
- the importance of estimating, e.g. in dividing 924 by 22, we could use 10 × 22 = 220 as a first step, but it would be worth progressing children onto estimating that 4 lots of 10 × 22 would be nearer 900, and a next step could be that 40 × 22 = 880.

Here, the number line is used as the basis for progression, from addition through its links with subtraction (or finding difference) and then using this understanding in multiplication and division. When progressing through to using negative integers, the same technique can still apply. Note, too, that the movement along the line is consistently from the smaller (sometimes zero) to the larger number, though of course when dealing with, say, –8 × 3, it might be better to visualise three steps moving in the negative direction.

The approach to calculation

To summarise, calculation is best addressed through enabling children to tackle problems mentally first, then, for more complex calculations, they can move on to informal presentations, such as the number line (or grid method for multiplication, illustrated below). Only when they fully understand what the calculation is about, and that they can use whatever method works for them, is it useful for them to attempt to learn the standard methods. For example, given the multiplication 23 × 15, the three processes discussed above can be illustrated as follows:

Mental method

23 × 15 = 23 × 10 + 23 × 5
23 × 10 = 230; 23 × 5 is half of this, so 23 × 5 = 115; 230 + 115 = 345

Many children, including those who have difficulties with mathematics, know how to multiply by 10. From this, the pattern that multiplying by 5 is half the result of multiplying by 10 can be established. These techniques can be practised as starters to the lessons. Clearly, other techniques will have to be adopted for multiplying by other numbers, such as multiplying by 4 and realising that this is equivalent to doubling and doubling again, but the key is that the confidence to handle numbers mentally is a crucial starting point in calculating.

Informal method

The common informal method for long multiplication is known as the grid or box method, where the numbers are partitioned (so that 23 becomes 20 and 3, and 15 becomes 10 and 5). The numbers are organised as in Figure 3.14.

×	20	3	
10	200	30	=230
5	100	15	=115
			345

Figure 3.14 The grid or box method for long multiplication

This method expands the calculation, making visible all its different parts. With a two-digit by two-digit multiplication, there are four mini-multiplications (20 × 10; 3 × 10; 20 × 5 and 3 × 5), each of which should be added together to make the total. Many children miss out some of the calculations, often multiplying the two units together, then the two amounts of tens, then adding.

Formal method (standard written algorithm)

In the standard presentation, these calculations are condensed, but it is worth making the comparison explicit to children who may just be able to use the method, so that they can see where the calculations come from. Note that this is the method specified in the KS3 curriculum. This comparison is shown in Figure 3.15.

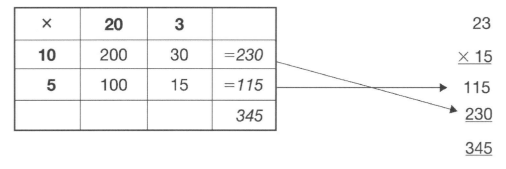

Figure 3.15 Comparing methods for multiplication

Translating ideas into different learning media

Mel Lever (2003) describes a visual representation of the months of the year as a clock face, or as a twelve-pointed star.

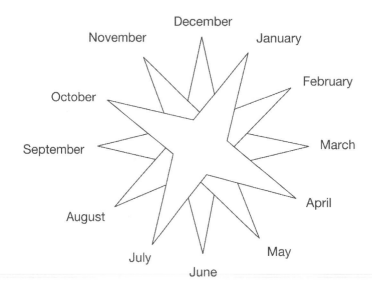

Figure 3.16 The cycle of months in the year in a visual (clock) form

Children could either use this visual representation to help understand the cycle of the year, and address questions about particular months or relationships between the months (e.g. 'Which months are six months apart?'), or they could place themselves physically in this arrangement. Other possibilities – dressing up appropriately for winter, spring, summer and autumn, and seating themselves in the right place – then come into play; relationships between seasons (spring and autumn being opposite) can be explored, and the cycle of the year (e.g. counting four months from November goes into the next year, or counting on a number of years) can be discussed.

It would be easy to assume that most information transmitted between children and their teacher is in auditory form, and that this type of learning occurs naturally in the normal course of events. However, there are activities that explicitly develop auditory skills, such as this visualisation script.

A visualisation script

The visualisation script given below is an example of a text that can be read to a class with the intention of developing children's capacity to translate information given in one form (auditory) to another form (visual). Children are only asked to imagine an image, and alter it as per the instructions. Such modelling is an essential mathematical skill in interpreting problems in order to solve them.

Expected responses from children are given in bold:

Objective

Classify triangles (isosceles, equilateral, scalene) using criteria such as equal sides, equal angles, lines of symmetry.

Script

Imagine a square. Draw the diagonals from the opposite corners. Ask:

- What shapes do you have inside the square? **Triangles**
- What do you know about these triangles? **Isosceles, congruent, identical, two sides the same, two angles the same, two angles are 45°, the other is 90°.**
- How do you know this?

Children could alternatively draw their images on individual whiteboards – translating the auditory information to their own diagrams, which can be easily displayed. This allows the teacher to assess the child's understanding quickly.

Changing resources to change the mathematics in an activity

Prestage and Perks (2001) describe how planning an activity with different resources changes the nature of the mathematics that can be learned from it. As a simple example, consider how children might find the mid-point along the base of a wall in the classroom.

If the resources they were offered (or that they chose) were a tape measure and (possibly) a calculator, then the mathematics to be learned might be:

*   Measure (and draw) lines to the nearest millimetre.
*   Use doubling and halving.
*   Check with inverse operations when using a calculator.
*   Identify the necessary information to solve a problem.

However, the mathematics will completely change if the resources offered to the children were only a stick (of no standard measurement, and without any calibrations) and perhaps a piece of string and a pencil, with which to find the mid-point of the base of the wall. Now the task is in the area of geometrical reasoning, because the solution lies in applying an understanding of symmetry. If pupils mark off several stick lengths, starting at each end of the wall, where they come to near the centre, they can then use the string between the two central marks, fold it in half and then lay it down to find the mid-point. The mathematics in this activity could be described through these objectives:

*   Identify the necessary information to solve a problem and represent problems and interpret solutions in geometric form.
*   Find simple loci, by reasoning.

In summary, considering different resources for different learning styles also opens up the opportunity for new and deeper understandings of mathematics to be explored.

Using colour

Colours can be used to emphasise or clarify patterns or links. For example, in helping children to develop their geometric reasoning skills, colours can highlight equal angles in sets of parallel lines (Figure 3.17).

Some questions that could accompany this activity might be:

*   Colour in all the angles that have the same value. Use a different colour for different sized angles.
*   How many different colours do you need?

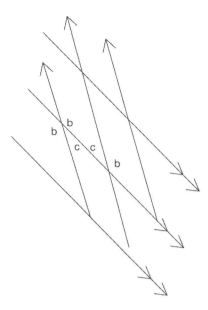

Figure 3.17 Two sets of parallel lines, to help children highlight the fact that vertically opposite, corresponding and alternate angles are equal

- Why only two?
- Does this have anything to do with the numbers of sets of parallel lines?

If a *third* set of parallel lines is added, which cut through the same points of intersection – how many colours are now needed?

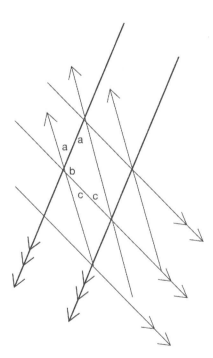

Figure 3.18 Three sets of parallel lines, to illustrate that the three angles in a triangle match the three angles on a straight line

By colouring differently the angles marked a, b and c, the connections between the angles on the straight line and the angles in a triangle are highlighted. This is an important mathematical idea, generated from the use of colour, to clarify relationships within parallel lines, leading to a proof that the angles in a triangle sum to 180°. Such techniques make this level of mathematical understanding far more accessible than formal written methods.

Physical movement can be used to understand mathematical ideas

The topic of angles and bearings can be addressed in this way. For instance, we can ask the class to face north (assuming that we know which direction that is from your classroom!). Children could then be asked to face the other points of the compass together; or to turn a specific number of degrees; or to face particular bearings. This can reinforce the idea that bearings represent a clockwise turn from north, and help children estimate a range of angles. This gives a physical experience that an angle is a measurement of turn.

An understanding of coordinates can also be addressed in a similar way. Organising the group into a block, and assigning each child with coordinates, useful questions can be asked to allow children to experience patterns and rules in coordinates, e.g.:

- Stand up (or hands up) if your first number (x coordinate) is 2.
- Stand up (or hands up) if your second number (y coordinate) is 3.
- Stand up (or hands up) if your numbers are the same.
- Stand up (or hands up) if your two numbers add up to 7.

Each of these will produce straight-line answers – children can recognise these connections from their experience.

Structuring thinking

Spider diagrams – moving from the known to the unknown

Another example of using a visual presentation to structure thinking is in the use of 'spider' diagrams or concept/mind maps. For example, using such a diagram (Figure 3.19) can build an understanding of finding decimal fractions of numbers. Starting from the centre, children could offer connected calculations and explain their links from the centre. Alternatively, the teacher could write in the link and ask children to calculate what should be the result.

These diagrams could be used in many areas of mathematics, e.g. to help children manipulate algebraic expressions (Appendix 20), or to make links between fractions or percentages.

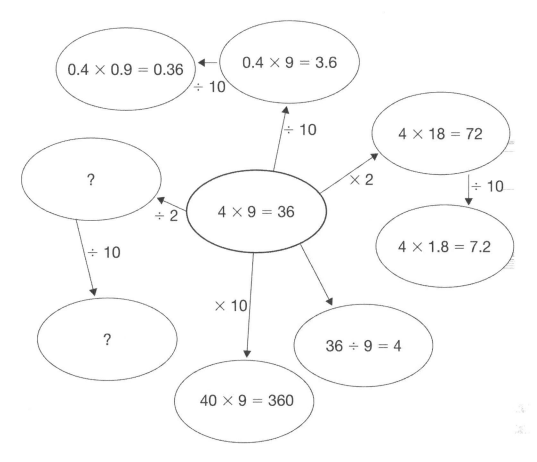

Figure 3.19 Spider diagram, using connections between whole numbers and decimals

Using tables to solve problems

Organising information is an important mathematical skill, but it is also an essential teaching technique to help children who have difficulties with their mathematics.

There are many problems that create links involving multiplication – conversion problems (metric to metric, metric to imperial, and currency problems), percentages, scale drawings, fractions, ratio and proportion problems, and enlargements are just a few examples. Often such problems are presented in words, and most examples of solutions offered in texts are also written. However, many children can be helped if they are shown how to organise the information given into tables, so that the links between the numbers are clarified, e.g.:

> With every £10 I can buy 15 euros for my trip to France. I manage to save £60 to use as spending money. How many euros can I buy?

Figure 3.20 shows how this information can be organised. Children should be asked about how to construct the table – what headings are needed, where to put the numbers 15 and 60, as well as what links the numbers. It is in the process of organising the problem that we find how to solve it.

	Pounds	Euros
	10	15
	60	

× 6   × 6

Figure 3.20 Using a table to help solve a currency conversion problem

The calculation is now clarified – children are helped to see why they have to multiply the number of euros by 6.

The problem can be extended, e.g.:

If I come back with 30 euros, how many pounds can I buy with this?'

The table is shown in Figure 3.21.

	Pounds	Euros
	10	15
	60	90
		30

× 2   × 2

Figure 3.21 Extending the problem

Another example of this approach is illustrated in Appendix 6, where the metric conversions (e.g. answering such questions as how many centimetres are in a metre, etc.) are displayed alongside the familiar 'HTU' – hundreds, tens and units presentation of place value. Children should be invited to see patterns and predict entries into the table. This clarifies the connections within the number system, and helps children see the consistency in the design of the metric measurement systems we use.

Structured writing/developing mathematical literacy

There is a distinction between the development of mathematical literacy and developing literacy skills through mathematics. Consider children explaining why the probability of getting a 'head' when tossing a coin is ½. The language needed to explain this might include 'fair', 'even', 'equally likely', 'outcome', and so on – vocabulary which can be strategically placed on display so that children may refer to it in their explanations. We might, after some discussion, ask children to try to convince someone (a pen friend, a parent, etc.) *in writing* that the probability is ½. Here is an opportunity to engage in the drafting process, to develop children's precision in using the vocabulary and capacity to construct a convincing argument – both of which are authentic tasks for mathematicians at any level.

The written pieces can be developed in a number of ways:

- The teacher could share some work for discussion (take photos, use a visualiser, copy examples, etc.). The class could together improve the writing and use of vocabulary.
- Children could pass their written pieces to each other, to see how well they understand each other's arguments. They could then review each other's work together and improve the writing.

Whichever method is used, it is founded on the drafting process to improve writing. Of course, ICT could be used effectively here. The messages sent out by doing this are:

- We cannot expect to master everything – including writing – at the first go (Mason 1988).
- The first written draft does not have to be perfect – indeed, it is unlikely to be so.
- The quality of our work improves through the process of review and redraft.

There is a danger, in attempting to develop literacy skills through mathematics, in considering low-level skills and applying them falsely to a mathematical context, for example an exercise for pupils could look like this:

Complete these sentences:

- The . . . . of tossing a coin and getting a head is ½.
- A head and a tail are equally likely . . . . from tossing a coin once.

These are simply written forms of the low-level 'guess what's in my head' questions, going little further than recalling knowledge of the particular words 'probability' (first sentence) and 'outcomes' (second sentence). Like many word searches, such activities do not develop an understanding of the vocabulary, and how it should be applied to describe or to explain or to convince someone of an argument, which is arguably the purpose of being literate. These are not authentic tasks for mathematicians and arguably do not help children *become* mathematicians.

If children genuinely have word-finding difficulties, it would be more effective for them to have ready and easy access to the vocabulary (either through display or through reference books or sheets) and a meaningful situation where they are required to use this vocabulary, such as in explaining their methods, describing shapes or patterns, justifying the rules they have discovered, or reasoning about a mathematical situation.

On the other hand, writing and speaking frames (as exemplified in Chapter 2 and Appendices 17 and 21) help children who have difficulties with mathematics to organise their thinking. These frames act as prompts to thinking about how children are going to solve problems, rather than testing recall of knowledge.

Teaching styles

The emphasis on an episodic structure enables teachers to employ a range of teaching styles to suit the objectives of the lesson and to use a varied palette of learning styles.

There are a number of ways in which teaching styles have been described, so some clarification of the terms is necessary. Both 'traditional' and 'progressive' descriptions have been used pejoratively at various times, and perhaps neither term is truly an adequate description of what goes on in mathematics classrooms.

This book promotes the idea that children learn through talk and action, characterised by purposeful collaboration and authentic, meaningful mathematical activities. If, in 'traditional' settings, children follow mechanistic routines and have limited opportunities to communicate their ideas – to exchange meaning – then the opportunities for understanding are similarly limited. Certainly, transmitting knowledge in a direct style is efficient and enables us to cover a curriculum, but there must be serious questions about whether children understand all that goes on. On the other hand, if in 'progressive' classrooms activities are not followed by purposeful reflection, and the teacher takes little responsibility for developing progression in understanding, then again the children's learning is restricted.

Quite simply, the best tack to take is to realise that different approaches or styles may be the most appropriate at certain times for certain pupils in certain situations. We should be looking to develop a repertoire of skills and approaches in the classroom: sometimes 'telling them' is both efficient and effective; other times children will need to handle mathematical equipment such as connecting cubes to understand a situation. Further opportunities to make links to other aspects of mathematics are essential – fractions and decimals form an integral part of understanding probability; exploring areas of rectangles can support an understanding of the commutative law of multiplication. Mathematics teachers will recognise when and how to make these links for individual pupils.

At the heart of considering teaching styles must lie an understanding of our values – not only what we believe about how children learn as described above in terms of talk and action, but also what it is they should learn. This latter point can be exemplified by considering the distinction between whether we are teaching children about mathematics (reflecting that the goal of learning is the acquisition of knowledge) or whether we are teaching children to become mathematicians (reflecting the participatory or situated model – 'learning and a sense of identity are inseparable', Lave and Wenger 1991). The former may lead us into believing that children learn through the transmission of knowledge; the latter may help us to recognise the importance of enabling children to handle mathematical vocabulary effectively in their own attempts at reasoning. Again, perhaps there is a place for both styles. However, if the inclusive classroom is one where children become empowered, then such empowerment can only come from developing their self-esteem, and this self-esteem arises from feeling that they understand, and that they belong in their community. On this view, coverage of a curriculum cannot be allowed to override an understanding of it.

4 Monitoring and assessment

The purposes of assessment

In designing any assessment system, it is important to be clear about its purposes. A conflict of audience interests can impair the value of the assessment itself. The following list provides a guide:

- to improve learning (by identifying both successes and misconceptions, and adjusting future teaching accordingly);
- to inform pupils of their progress;
- to inform parents of pupils' progress;
- school and teacher accountability.

Assessment systems intended to inform parents of pupil progress should look quite different from the methods of informing children. Children will need guidance on specific objectives, often on a day-to-day basis, and such advice may form part of plenary sessions of mathematics lessons, or comments when marking books. Such detail may not be necessary for parents, who may want a larger picture of progress, and therefore advice on more general ways they can help their children. Parents may be more interested in levels or grades but, as Black and Wiliam (1998) suggest in their discussion of formative assessment, these may be counter-productive when discussing progress with children. This will be dealt with more fully later in the chapter.

Useful documentation for understanding progression

There are four key documents in supporting progression and assessment, available for teachers in England:

- Performance – P Scale (DfE 2014b);
- Mathematics Programmes of Study: Key Stages 1 and 2 (DfE 2013c);
- Mathematics Programmes of Study: Key Stage 3 (DfE 2013b);
- Mathematics Programmes of Study: Key Stage 4 (DfE 2014a).

The first document presents statements about what pupils are able to do prior to achieving standards of work associated with the national curriculum, while the latter three present the age-related expectations for pupils in Years 1–11. These can therefore be used in conjunction to identify progression (see Chapter 2) and can support the development of an assessment system.

In 2014 a government decision was made to move away from using NC levels, often referred to as 'life after levels' or 'assessment without levels'. This has muddied the waters concerning assessment for some, but if we refer back to the purposes of assessment (at the beginning of this chapter) it is clear that NC levels are not required to meet any of these objectives. As long as the assessment has a clear purpose and the teacher has a good understanding of the way in which pupils progress with their learning, then more meaningful assessment is possible.

How we assess

The latest National Curriculum offers no guidance on how the content should be assessed, placing it in the hands of the teacher to formulate a useful assessment policy. However, the now outdated *Framework for Teaching Mathematics: Years 7, 8 and 9* (DfES 2001) still offers good advice on how to maximize the impact of assessment; it states that:

> Where *assessment* is concerned, better standards of mathematics occur when:
>
> - pupils understand and are engaged in the assessment process;
> - teachers use pupils' contributions to assess their strengths and difficulties, to set group and individual targets for pupils to achieve and to plan the next stage of work;
> - assessments include informal observations, oral questioning and occasional tests or special activities designed to judge progress;
> - recording systems give teachers the information that they need to plan and report successfully, but are not too time-consuming to maintain.

Our assessment of children's work is conducted through written and oral forms, both informally and through formal testing.

Informal observations/oral questioning

The quality of these assessments is directly related to the quality and nature of the questioning. Here is the classification by Berger *et al.* (2000) again, detailing the aims of questioning:

- recalling facts;
- applying facts;
- hypothesising and predicting;
- designing and comparing procedures;
- interpreting;
- applying reasoning.

Clearly, questions limited to the 'What is 6 × 8?' type only assess recall. A greater range of questions (such as those presented in Appendix 18) will offer teachers a better insight into children's understanding, and then enable teachers to think of learning activities that develop children's understanding further. The example given below of a lesson about finding percentages illustrates how such questioning can emerge from considering a problem-solving approach to teaching.

Although the plenary session of structured mathematics lessons is specifically designed to enable informal assessments to take place regularly, it must be remembered that such questioning should take place throughout the various lesson episodes. Effective starters will reveal issues; teachers' or TAs' questions of individual pupils in the main activities will reveal misconceptions that can be addressed in whole-class discussions.

Marking, using formative assessment effectively in the classroom, and the impact of the choice of activity on assessment

Black and Wiliam (1998) argue that improving learning through assessment depends on:

- the provision of effective feedback to pupils;
- the active involvement of pupils in their own learning;
- adjusting teaching to take account of the results of assessment;
- a recognition of the profound influence assessment has on the motivation and self-esteem of pupils, both of which are crucial influences on learning;
- the need for pupils to be able to assess themselves and understand how to improve.

These considerations are true for all pupils.

It is also important to keep in mind that in just the same way that the quality of learning is directly affected by the choice of activity (Chapter 3, 'Know and use the order of operations' lesson), so the quality of our feedback to pupils is also affected by the nature of the activity we are assessing. The following example illustrates this point.

Method 1
To find a percentage of a quantity, you can change the percentage into a
fraction or a decimal and multiply this by the quantity, e.g.:

Find 48% of 250
48% = 0.48. So 0.48 x 250 = 120

Calculate the following:
(i) 45% of 220   (ii) 22% of 50 kg   (iii) 75% of £480

Figure 4.1 Teaching percentages of a quantity from a given method

Children are often given pages of this sort of exercise, perhaps because of the
belief that practising a given method ensures learning. However, this kind of
presentation of the problem does not ensure understanding of what finding a
percentage of a quantity means, and more importantly it does not help children
understand how to apply the knowledge they already have. For example, they
may already be confident in their own mental strategies for these calculations,
by using the method shown later in this section (Figure 4.2).

What are the likely ways in which this exercise in Figure 4.1 would be marked
or assessed? Some possibilities are described below:

- A page of ticks or crosses, presented as a fraction of correct answers, e.g. 7
  out of 10. Note Black and Wiliam's (1998) concern that 'greater attention given
  to marking and grading, much of it tending to lower the self-esteem of pupils,
  rather than to providing advice for improvement and a strong emphasis on
  comparing pupils with each other which demoralises the less successful
  learners' are *inhibiting* factors to effective learning. This type of marking could
  also contribute to more 'fixed mindset' in pupils (see Dweck 2007).
- Constructive comments – perhaps linked to how the pupils have attempted
  to use the method. This may be better but can only be considered formative if children have an opportunity to apply their response to the comments
  as soon as possible. If such marking has taken place at the end of the work,
  the comments may not even be read, let alone used to improve learning,
  and the effort could be wasted.
- Comments related to children's presentation. Black and Wiliam (1998) also
  cite 'a tendency for teachers to assess quantity of work and presentation
  rather than the quality of learning' as another inhibiting factor for effective
  learning.

However, if we contrast this presentation of the task with an activity that is
designed to build children's problem-solving strategies as well as their skills
in handling percentages, we can immediately see that the 'quality of learning'
to which Black and Wiliam refer is enhanced.

Beginning with the centre of a spider diagram, a process can be modelled for pupils for finding percentages of the given number. This spider is illustrated in Figure 4.2.

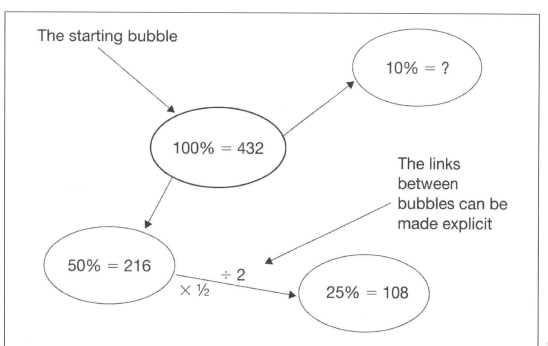

Pupils can be organised into pairs, and invited to make up their own spider diagram of percentages from a new starting quantity. They can be challenged to find as many percentages of this quantity as they can.

In the plenary session pupils can be asked to apply their findings for a range of quantities and percentages, e.g. present a table such as this:

Percentage	Quantity
25%	£6
15%	50g
1%	260
54%	45 miles

Combining any percentage with any quantity (there are 16 different questions here), children can be asked to find the solution, and explain how they worked it out. The assessment that takes place here is immediate, and focused *not just on the answer, but also on the method of calculating*.

Figure 4.2 A spider diagram method for presenting percentages of quantities

However, the key question 'What is a good percentage to work with?' takes the lesson to another aspect of mathematics – examining strategies for solving problems. Given the objectives:

- solve problems involving the calculation of percentages (Y6), or
- interpret percentages (KS3)

there is a danger of presenting children with an activity that only addresses these objectives in narrow ways, such as that given in Figure 4.1. However, the presentation in Figure 4.2 goes further, involving objectives taken from the 'Solve Problems' section of the KS3 National Curriculum such as:

- develop their mathematical knowledge, in part through solving problems and evaluating the outcomes, including multi-step problems;
- make and use connections between different parts of mathematics to solve problems.

This lesson works on the premise that children will learn effectively through engaging in an activity where they are part of the decision-making (they choose which percentages to find), where they work collaboratively in deciding and calculating, and where their engagement leads them to understand strategies for finding *any* percentage of *any* quantity. The key question highlights the strategy children are likely to use, and enables them to be clear about their problem-solving techniques. This is much more of a learning activity than giving the answers to a page of an exercise.

Black and Wiliam (1998) assert that:

> Feedback to any pupil should be about the particular qualities of his or her work, with advice on what he or she can do to improve, and should avoid comparisons with other pupils.

Therefore, in implementing formative assessment techniques in the classroom, it is essential to keep in mind what we can be formative *about*. In the example given above, the assessment of children's work can be focused on their 'mathematical performance' – how they go about solving the problems – rather than on written outcomes (answers) to a page of questions. So, in finding a percentage of a given quantity, the mathematical performance rests on a range of skills:

Table 4.1 Identifying the skills used within a specific problem

Generic problem-solving skills	Skills specific to this problem
Clarifying the problem	By, for example, translating the problem to a number line, or other diagrammatic or physical representation. By identifying the key meanings from the problem, e.g. that finding a percentage less than 100% gives an answer less than the original, and greater than 100% gives an answer that is greater than the original quantity.
Breaking the problem down into smaller, manageable parts	Breaking the percentage down into a series of manageable calculations.
Identifying the techniques needed to solve the problem	Possible techniques include: • applying an understanding that *'of'* relates to multiplying; • choosing to use fractions, decimals or percentage equivalents – e.g. '33⅓% of £12' is better translated into '⅓ of £12' to make a more efficient calculation; • understanding that the value can be expressed as multiples of 10% + a multiple of 1%; • understanding that the percentage can be expressed as a combination of other, easily calculable percentages, e.g. 26% = 25% + 1%.
Fluency	Doing the calculations accurately and efficiently: • applying any of a range of appropriate calculating skills, e.g. halving quantities to find 50%, halving again for 25%; • applying the understanding that finding 10% of a quantity is equivalent to dividing it by 10; • dividing quantities by 10 and 100, by recognising the change in place value; • finding multiples of 10% or 1%, and combining these results.
Strategic fluency, e.g.: • using tables of results, to establish links; • finding patterns in results to predict later outcomes; • using estimation to help decide the strategy for working, and for checking; • choosing tools to assist, e.g. using a calculator for efficiency; checking	Estimating percentages, e.g. 48% of 220 must be just less than half of 220, about 110. A table of results could be: | 100%	220
10%	22
50%	110
25%	55
1%	2.2
24% (25% − 1%)	52.8 (55 − 2.2)
48% (24% × 2)	105.6 (52.8 × 2)	

Table 4.1 continued

Generic problem-solving skills	Skills specific to this problem
	Finding ways of checking, e.g. translating percentages to fractions/decimals, estimating answers, using a calculator, finding alternative routes to an answer.
Evaluating the process	Evaluating the collaboration: • How did we work together? • What roles did we take? • Were decisions made jointly? Evaluating problem-solving techniques: Would working with fractions be easier sometimes? E.g. for 33⅓% it would be easier to find ⅓ of the total instead of going through 10%, 1% and ⅓%.

When feeding back information to pupils, therefore, we can analyse how they attempt to solve the problem, and then identify the steps they need to take to improve.

In this case, it may be that the child has difficulty right at the start in clarifying what to do to solve the problem. It may also be that involving the child in translating the problem to a visual form, such as a number line, will help, e.g. 'Find 40% of 220' (see Figure 4.3).

The number line can be used for counting in twenty-twos to reach 40%; it provides a visual illustration of what needs to be found.

Perhaps translating the problem into a table (as at the bottom of Table 4.1) would be an alternative, because it means that children are guided to find the salient information from the text.

The first question has to be 'What do you have to find out?', followed by 'Can you present this information another way?' If the child is still stuck, then there are clear teaching points illustrated; perhaps first address how they might translate ideas into number lines or tables.

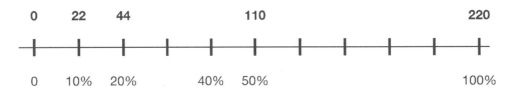

Figure 4.3 Using a number line to represent a percentages problem

The marking of this type of work takes a different form from ticks and crosses and a mark out of ten. Here, we are led directly into making constructive comments, without the need for grades or marks. These comments will be related to structuring or scaffolding how the child goes about solving the problem; e.g. if they can tabulate results, can they then use the information to find links? Can they use the links to predict later numbers?

Pupil involvement

For children who have difficulties with their mathematics, formative assessment can be used as a powerful motivating force. Children who can clearly see *how* they are making progress enjoy their successes and are encouraged to sustain their efforts.

Part of the process is to engage children in assessing for themselves. This can be achieved through self-assessment or peer assessment. Conducted regularly, this process can help children understand more clearly what they have to do to succeed, and reflect on the ways in which they are working more effectively.

The lesson described above could take on an element of pupil self-assessment or peer assessment. The teacher, TA or pupil partners could ask which aspects of solving the problem they found hard, perhaps using the identification offered in Table 4.1 as a guideline. Children would become clearer themselves about how they are working and what progress they are making with regular exposure to the generic problem-solving statements:

- clarifying the problem;
- breaking the problem down into manageable parts;
- identifying the appropriate techniques to solve the problem;
- fluency;
- evaluating the process.

When planning a specific task, the teacher may find it useful to produce a bespoke progression grid; this shows what success at various levels of difficulty might look like across the generic problem-solving statements (see the example in Appendix 22). With pupils, teacher and TA in possession of a progression grid, the assessment process could then take the following forms:

- As pupils are working on longer investigational or problem-solving tasks, the teacher (or TA) could discuss with pupils what they have achieved in their work, indicating this achievement on the criteria sheet. Targets could quickly be identified, either by using the criterion from the next level or by looking at another strand.

- Pupils could attempt to assess their own work using the criteria. This mark could be compared with the teacher's assessment, and differences discussed. This process clarifies the criteria, and what constitutes evidence for achieving them.
- Pupils could mark each other's work. This process requires pupils to justify their assessments, which again develops their understanding of the criteria and their requirements. However, this process also needs to be monitored, and it may prove more useful once pupils have gained a certain amount of experience with the criteria.

Using these criteria will expose pupils to the more open-ended problem-solving type questions that are becoming more prevalent in the new GCSE (particularly Assessment Objective 3 and to a lesser extent Assessment Objective 2). The process can be adopted throughout Key Stage 3 as well as Key Stage 4 to help support pupils to solve longer mathematical problems successfully, and such use of the assessment criteria means that we are teaching children these processes effectively.

There is a further development of pupil self-assessment in the next section.

What do we assess?

The answer to this question is not confined to problem-solving strategies alone.

It is useful to record pupils' performance on a medium-term basis (either half-termly or termly). This usually fits well with whole-school data collections and, given that there is no desire to duplicate work, this seems prudent. As for what is recorded, that is for the school and the individual teachers/departments to agree on.

With the move towards mastery and the absence of levels, some system of matching pupils' progress up against some key objectives seems to be the favoured method for most schools during this period of transition. Examples of methods include:

- Level Ladders – A specific objective is shown at various levels of difficulty and a pupil is placed on a particular rung.
- Assessing Pupil Progress Grids – The columns contain different areas of mathematics (e.g. number, algebra, etc.), while the rows represent particular skills within those areas, increasing in difficulty as you move through the rows. Pupil performance can be noted against particular skills using a ✓/✗ or some sort of grading system.
- Personalised Learning Checklists – An exam is analysed in such a way that a pupil ends with a list of skills they have succeeded in and a list of those that they are yet to master.

These systems all present a marked benefit over awarding a more traditional grade or level, as they give some indication as to what the pupil needs to do in order to progress with their learning. There is no need for a separate target-setting process as it is integrated into the assessment. Although these systems may be useful for the majority of pupils working in the expected attainment range for the year group, any system based on objectives may not appear so appropriate for children experiencing difficulties. For example, a key objective in KS3 is:

> Use the four operations, including formal written methods, applied to integers, decimals, proper and improper fractions, and mixed numbers, all both positive and negative.

For some children with difficulties, 'developing mental or informal strategies for the four operations' may be a clearer and more appropriate objective. However, this is not to dismiss the key objectives for children with SEND, because they form a basis of entitlement. Our task is to find ways to address them meaningfully in our classrooms.

The problem for a teacher of children experiencing difficulties with mathematics is that the range of objectives appropriate for the class is likely to be very broad, taking in objectives from P levels through to those working at their current age-related expectations. This will have the likely effect of producing an assessment system that is too large to manage. It may be worth considering an assessment system focused on the *likely* areas of difficulty, so that we can identify children's progression with the most fundamental aspects of mathematics.

Berger *et al.* (2000) identified the following key mathematical concepts for children with learning difficulties, especially at Key Stage 2:

- number, including cardinality and ordinality;
- counting, including one-to-one correspondence;
- operation of combining and partitioning;
- comparing two numbers;
- concepts of length, mass, capacity, time and money;
- comparing two quantities;
- classification of 2D and 3D shapes;
- mathematical pattern;
- concept of having properties or attributes;
- classification by criteria;
- position, direction and movement.

These concepts form the basis of an understanding of number, but some also encourage an understanding in other aspects of mathematics. For example, an understanding of mathematical pattern will show itself in work on shape and space, such as tessellations and symmetry, but it is also an important feature of algebra – number sequences – and in handling data the concept is further developed in looking at trends in graphs and tables.

At Key Stages 3 and 4 the specified curriculum is wider, with a greater emphasis on problem-solving, algebra, handling data and ratio and proportion, and we should also consider the following concepts as major objectives in understanding mathematics:

- complements to 'useful' numbers, e.g. 10, 100, 1000 and multiples of these; also to 0.1 and 1 when calculating with decimals;
- place value, linked with the effect of multiplying by 10, 100, 1000 and decimal fractions;
- multiples – the times tables; and linked with this
- the relationships between the four arithmetic operations, and the links to algebra;
- using appropriate vocabulary to describe mathematical situations; and
- applying effective strategies to solve problems.

The latter two concepts do not imply discrete lessons. The effective use of vocabulary and the application of problem-solving strategies should become a feature of all lessons but, since assessment tends to drive the curriculum, it is important to highlight their place in an assessment system.

It is suggested that those children who have difficulties in their mathematics tend to have difficulties in some or all of the concepts described. It seems sensible that, whichever system you are using to record pupil performance, students who are experiencing difficulties use a system that enables them to understand how they are achieving against these key concepts. Concepts may be added or removed – it is not suggested that this is a comprehensive list, but merely a guideline for consideration.

Pupil self-assessment

When a ladder, grid, personalised learning checklist or some other method of recording progress against objectives is used, it serves to enable pupils to reflect on their learning. It is common to use a 'traffic light' system; children indicate if they are confident that they understand (green), not quite sure (amber) or 'don't get it at all' (red). Other schools use a numbered system in a similar way (e.g. 1 = confident, 2 = not sure and 3 = do not understand), or qualitative categories such as 'beginning', 'secure' and 'mastered'. Whichever method of feedback is used, pupils' responses will be most honest, and therefore most useful to the teacher, if there has been discussion about its purpose.

Creating an environment where learners can admit to their lack of understanding without 'losing face' is a key component for effective self-assessment. The most useful statements to reflect upon will be the main teaching objectives from lessons over a term/half-term, or any key objectives that have been assessed. When children have to deal with the objectives and the language within them in this way, it provides another opportunity for them to understand what the language means, and clarifies what they have to do to succeed.

Qualifications and examinations, GCSE, alternative accreditation

Any discussion about alternative accreditation must first address the question of expectations. The GCSE was established as a way of identifying achievement for the vast majority of pupils – many of whom would have statements for special educational needs, or education, health and care (EHC) plans as they are now termed. There are very few children for whom the GCSE Mathematics course is inappropriate. As a guide, the new GCSE grade 1 is roughly equivalent to the old National Curriculum level 3/4 (which historically was achieved or bettered by ≈94% of students at KS2). Given a further five years of education, it is clear that there should be few pupils who remain working beneath this standard. Mapping the new KS2 scaled scores is more of an unknown, but it seems reasonable to assume that a similarly small percentage of pupils will be unable to access the GCSE as we go forward.

The Mathematics Entry Level Certificates provide an option for those that are unable to access the GCSE; however, one should remember there are children who achieve below the expected level at KS2/3 but still pass a GCSE in KS4. It is hard work, but these successes are significant features of many schools throughout the country.

Entry Level qualifications

The levels of challenge of these qualifications are broadly in line with the old National Curriculum levels 1, 2 and 3. The qualifications available at this level include basic skills such as adult literacy and numeracy as well as National Curriculum subjects such as English, science and mathematics. These qualifications are therefore applicable to a wide range of people, from 14 years old to adult, including those with SEND. The courses are run in schools, often as a one- or two-year programme in Years 10 and 11, but they are also run in residential care settings, prisons, young offenders' institutions and FE colleges.

Entry level certificates vary as to whether they are assessed internally or externally; one should consider the qualification/exam board and select one that uses an assessment structure that is suitable for the child that is sitting it.

Special arrangements or considerations for examinations

This is the source of many dilemmas for teachers, as well as quite a lot of paperwork. There are pupils who will clearly struggle in an examination setting, and for many it may be that they have such difficulty with reading the questions that their chance of doing the mathematics is inhibited.

Pupils are entitled to special arrangements if it can be shown that the process of assessment through examinations inhibits their capacity to demonstrate their ability within the subject. For example, those pupils who have a specific learning difficulty, which perhaps shows itself in being unable to read questions from a paper independently, yet have throughout their school careers demonstrated high levels of mathematical understanding, are entitled to special arrangements. These must be appropriate for the child, and within that child's experience. The child might therefore just need extra time, may need a larger print version of the paper, or may need a reader or a scribe. Whatever support they have for the examination, it is essential that the child has had previous experience of it, i.e. in a similar situation (e.g. internal examinations) or it represents their regular way of working. It is also important that formal application is made to the examining board in plenty of time for arrangements to be made.

Clearly the corollary to this is that if the examination setting does not unduly inhibit the child's capacity to demonstrate understanding, then special arrangements are not applicable. If the child's reading, problem-solving and mathematical skills are all weak, then the examination will demonstrate this, and it will do so fairly.

> For further details see: Access Arrangements, Reasonable Adjustments and Special Consideration, www.jcq.org.uk/exams-office/access-arrangements-and-special-consideration

Preparing pupils for tests and examinations

There is much we can do to help pupils with SEND prepare for any examinations or tests. Revising for mathematics is most effective through developing experience at problem-solving. It involves a range of skills – extracting information, translating this into another meaningful form, selecting an appropriate operation or other mathematical technique and checking results. As Mason (1988) points out: 'It is virtually impossible to read mathematics – it has to be done, to be worked through with pencil and paper.' This is certainly true of revision, and so the best revision technique is to regularly look at test questions and discuss them with pupils, so that they can unravel their meanings and make their own decisions about solving them. Certain techniques have proved successful for many teachers in the past, including:

- Regular extra sessions, staffed by both teachers and teaching assistants, focused on solving test questions. These sessions could be during registration times, after school or at lunchtimes. Some schools hold Saturday sessions for pupils, and these have the effect of raising the status of the examinations. For some children, getting them to believe that the qualifications have a genuine value is an important step.
- Special event days – again either on Saturdays, during holiday periods or as a planned whole day within school time, staffed by mathematics teachers and assistants, focused on how we solve the problems.

The main feature of both of these types of event is that children *discuss how to solve the problem*. There is little value in setting up these situations if the child then has to engage with a test paper individually and silently and without support. Through discussion, children begin to know what they know, and will be more likely to demonstrate that understanding independently in the real examination.

5 Managing support and intervention

The role of a teaching assistant

Traditionally a TA was seen as someone who sat alongside pupils within the classroom to help them access the work; although this type of work still has much merit, the role of a TA has continued to develop. The professional standards for teaching assistants (UNISON *et al*. 2016) state that 'the primary role of the teaching assistant should be to work with teachers to raise the learning and attainment of pupils while also promoting their independence, self-esteem and social inclusion'. This broad remit does not exclude the more traditional TA work but widens it to include activities such as pre-teaching topics, running extraction groups and developing resources.

Alongside this development in role, a number of job titles have emerged to describe staff who support teaching and learning, e.g. HLTAs (higher level TAs), special needs support staff, curriculum support staff, inclusion team assistants. In this chapter, the term TA will be used to represent all staff supporting teaching and learning.

Promoting self-esteem and social inclusion

At their most basic, the ideas about developing good self-esteem and social inclusion within mathematics education are mainly concerned with maximising a pupil's ability to participate in a lesson/session.

TAs can play an important role in facilitating access to activities, through support with:

- *organisation* – being prepared for the lesson/homework; structuring problem-solving;
- *the use of mathematical equipment* – e.g. calculators, protractors, compasses, etc.;
- *reading and interpreting written material* – part of the process of solving problems is to understand them, and children may understand written

problems better if they are helped to create diagrams or physical interpretations of the problems;

- *taking notes from the board*;
- *supporting pupils in contributing to class discussions* – often pupils like to validate their responses to an adult before speaking out to the whole class;
- *keeping pace with the lesson* – TAs could help children with setting out their work if this aspect holds up the pace of their learning. If, for instance, drawing out the framework of a table of results is not the objective for learning, but its completion prevents the child engaging with the real work, a TA could speed up the process by helping to set the table out.

Fox and Halliwell (2000) also suggest that the TA can help by:

- helping the pupils understand the sequence needed to complete the task (being careful that the learning is not defined by completion!). The goal is participation, and often this will conflict with a goal of 'having a completed product'.
- helping the pupil in knowing where to find relevant information (and how to use it);
- helping the pupil to catch up with missed work.

If the goals for participation are concerned with acting socially, efforts in planning need to be made to identify effective groups, and also the purposes for their collaboration. TAs should have a role in this planning and then in helping children with this socialisation, such as modelling taking turns to speak and listening to others.

If the support is during a lesson, depending on the size of the class, the TA could be involved in supervising the work of one (or more) group(s) while the teacher manages other groups. Mathematics activities such as problem-solving or extended investigations would fit well into this model, because the purposes of the collaboration centre on joint problem-solving.

If a teacher and a TA are working in a shared space, it is essential to remember that the teacher should be modelling the questioning and the behaviour management strategies for the classroom for the TA. Essential aspects of classroom management – keeping children on task, spotting early signs of disruption – are shared. This again implies that the role of the TA in that classroom has been clearly defined and agreed, so that both teacher and TA know how each should act in any given situation. This is an act of empowerment for the TA; responsibilities are shared, and there should be a mutual respect for the role of each adult.

Assessment and evaluation

The TA's role is different from that of the teacher and therefore offers a valuable alternative perspective on learning. Joint evaluations of the success of any activities during a lesson can be discussed, perhaps in relation to specific pupils. Furthermore, from other sessions or just by working closely with a pupil, the TA may have a clearer insight into how they tackled a problem, and could therefore illustrate misconceptions or flaws in children's methods. If TAs regularly place quickly made comments on 'sticky notes' inside pupils' books or folders, this can also be valuable in helping the teacher to understand any difficulties a pupil had, and how much assistance was given in completing a piece of work. These different types of feedback make planning for subsequent lessons more effective.

Promoting independence

Independence has long been a goal of teachers of children with SEND. It may be further described as being able to solve problems, being able to cope or succeed in all aspects of learning independently. If seen with these perspectives, it becomes clear that the link to pupil participation is strong, but also independence is concerned with developing the pupil's capacity for decision-making.

Decision-making by pupils can be inhibited or enhanced by the type of activities through which children learn their mathematics (note the percentage activity in Chapter 4) and also by the types of discussion with which the child engages with teachers or assistants. It is essential that both teachers and TAs are clear about the kinds of questioning which will enable children to make their own decisions about their mathematics. Too often we feel pressure to help children solve particular problems or 'finish their work' – especially  by false deadlines like the bell at the end of the lesson – and then we fall back on 'giving children methods that work'.

It is even more difficult to allow children experiencing difficulties with their mathematics the space and time to articulate their own ideas about how they could solve problems; but if they are regularly given a complete structure by adults and only have to engage with the *mechanics* of calculations, then they cannot achieve 'independence'. Greater independence is achieved through *increased* participation in the activities of mathematicians; mathematicians make their own (independent) decisions about which information to collect, which calculations to make, how to present their results, and so on. The notion that understanding can be deferred, i.e. that children mechanically process methods they are given, with the hope that at some later stage in their lives they will come to understand, is simply a deferring of one's responsibility to help children understand.

All the examples offered in these chapters illustrate how we help children understand their mathematics, whether it is the *structure* of the mathematics (e.g. understanding the number system by the use of number lines) or the *purposes* of it (e.g. looking at misleading graphs and charts to identify why we present information in certain ways).

To develop children's independence, therefore, also requires teachers and TAs to be clear about the stages of problem-solving – it is through this analysis that we can best find specific targets for children's learning (see Chapter 4).

An example of how different kinds of conversations which surround children's problem-solving affect the development of their independence could be seen as follows:

Problem – to find a way of adding 14 + 16.

The child is stuck on this problem.

Table 5.1 Version A – questions that keep the child dependent on support for learning

Conversation	Commentary
Adult: You can write the sum down like this: 14 +16	Already, the adult takes the first decision. Is the child ready for standard column addition? Does the child understand what addition means? Does the child recognise patterns in, say, 4+6, 14+6, 14+16, and could therefore be encouraged to tackle this mentally?
What's the answer to six add four?	The child may or may not respond accurately, but if finding complements to ten is not the difficulty, then it may be that the child's difficulty lies in understanding the problem, or setting it out in a form that the child understands, or in other aspects of calculating, e.g. what to do with the extra ten. It may be better to focus questions on these aspects, rather than only getting children involved at this mechanical level.

Table 5.1 continued

Conversation	Commentary

Well done! 4+6 is 10, so we put the zero down here and carry the one.
 	
  14
+16
   0
   1
	Here, the decision about setting out the sum has again been taken away from the child, so there can be no analysis of the child's understanding of where to place the zero or the ten. Many children reverse the digits, as if they are writing 10 in the wrong order:
	
	  14
	+16
	   1
	   0
	
	This can be dealt with more effectively when we ask the questions 'Where should we place the digits of 10?' and 'Why should we put them in these places?'

Good! What's three ones? So we can put the three there –
 	
  14
+16
  30
   1
	It's not three ones – it's three tens. It's no wonder some children have difficulties with numbers if they are regularly described incorrectly.

Some questions need addressing:

- What role has the child played in this activity?
- To what extent has the child participated in solving the problem?

Table 5.2 Version B – questions that develop independent thinking

Conversation	Commentary
Adult: What does the problem say? What do you think you have to work out? Can you use a diagram or equipment to help you, e.g. a number line?	The stages of problem-solving can offer a guideline for questioning. Understanding the problem – extracting useful data, knowing what it is that has to be found, translating the problem into another medium, e.g. visual form using a number line. Planning the problem, e.g. knowing what calculations to use, finding how the problem can be broken down into manageable parts. Doing the calculations. Evaluating/checking.

Conversation	Commentary
Where should you place the 14 on the number line?	The adult of course must make decisions about how much scaffolding to offer – if the child has no clue about some of the tools to use, it may be necessary to remind them of number lines, Diene's blocks, Numicon or counting sticks. However, the questions may still be asked so that children could make decisions about how to use them in their calculations.
How could you show that you are adding 16 on this number line?	
How could you use these (Diene's) blocks to show 14? How could you add 16?	
What other ways could we do this calculation?	There are a range of methods, e.g. the mental ones, including partitioning $14 + 16 = 10 + 4 + 10 + 6$ and reordering $= 10 + 10 + 4 + 6 = 10 + 10 + 10 = 30$
How can we check if the result is correct?	By using alternative methods or by reversing the calculation: $30 - 16 = 14$
Which method is best for you?	

These questions clearly demand a wide-ranging understanding of the subject, as well as a good working relationship with the child. The expectations of the standard of a TA's work are very high on this model. Such a model may also imply:

- The teachers in the mathematics department model the questioning techniques – therefore a high percentage of the TA's time is spent in class with mathematics teachers, to expedite the TA's professional development.
- Lessons are carefully planned together; TA feedback on how a child has fared with the stages of problem-solving is an essential planning tool for future lessons.

Raising standards of achievement for all pupils

If TA contracts are managed effectively, their hours could be organised to increase pupil contact with adults. Opportunities can be created for extra sessions at lunchtimes, after school, by extracting pupils from other lessons or during registration times for specific support. That support could take many forms, with examples including: spending time with Year 11 children to discuss examination paper questions, one-to-one support for children on specific mathematical targets, perhaps making use of 'concrete' materials such as Cuisenaire rods, or using some of the excellent software available to ensure understanding and enable learners to move on.

TA time could also be used for developing resources for learning, e.g. posters on the different types of graphs or charts children could use to present results, along with the reasons for their choices, or other posters as per Appendices 4–10. Other resources can be developed specifically for individual children, addressing their particular needs and improving their access to learning. Time needs to be allocated for this purpose, and therefore TAs need not be timetabled full-time in classes.

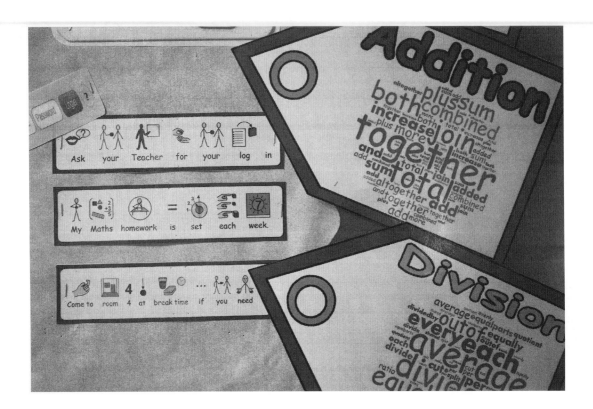

Managing the support – a whole-school view

The main focus lies in the planning of the support (in class or outside of it), identifying the amount of staff hours that are required to provide it, and then the school taking the decision to employ those staff members from its overall budget. This gives a clear indication by the school of its commitment to the support and how it should be deployed; there should also be a clear commitment to developing the qualities of its entire staff. Effective management of the support team should be concerned with developing TA expertise so as to best support a wide range of children. This expertise falls into two clear strands – subject knowledge and knowledge of the pupils who need support.

If TAs are deployed within departmental/subject areas, then clearly the responsibilities for development of subject knowledge lie here. The issue then, however, may be that neither the teaching staff nor the TAs have a holistic view of the child and how she/he copes in other subject areas. There may not be opportunities to see how colleagues in other departments use strategies that are effective with the pupil, and therefore limited scope for developing TAs' expertise. These issues can be addressed by ensuring regular opportunities for TAs and teachers to discuss and evaluate teaching strategies for particular children, and by support staff being afforded time for their own team meetings with the SENCO to share experiences and ideas about the strategies and resources that work well for different learners.

Conversely, if TAs are associated with particular pupils or year groups, there are clear benefits for developing their understanding of individuals. This in-depth knowledge will enable them to advise teaching staff on appropriate teaching strategies and resources; they can contribute to review meetings with pupils and parents, and they can feed these views back to teachers. However, their experience will be *across* the curriculum, and the development of their own subject knowledge will be inhibited. The onus will then be on maths teachers to communicate teaching strategies effectively with TAs. A contact sheet might be useful, enabling the teacher to share the structure, objectives and key questions of the lesson, and offering an opportunity for the TA to feed back any useful comments about pupils' experiences, to inform future planning. Even more effective, short training sessions with TAs supporting maths lessons can be provided (by the head of department perhaps) to ensure that they understand the teaching methods and processes being used. This will empower TAs, make them more confident and ensure that their support is of the highest quality.

The success of any model of managing support rests on working in partnership and cultivating mutual professional respect. The learning environment we seek to create works for everyone within it – primarily for the pupils, but also for the teachers and the TAs. The inclusive, problem-solving classroom includes us all; the problem we are solving is 'How can we best help our children learn effectively?' The partnership with TAs is a valuable tool with which to solve that problem.

6 Real pupils in real classrooms

Introduction

Although the previous chapters offer many examples of useful questions, activities and resources that can be used in the mathematics classroom, the real task is applying these ideas to children's learning. Here follow some brief case studies, each focusing on a particular area of special educational need, through which the techniques discussed in the previous chapters are exemplified. Each one follows the same format with three sections: 'You will need to find out', 'You should consider' and 'Some strategies you/the TA could try'.

Teachers may find these examples useful to promote discussion in team meetings, either as a mathematics team or in discussions between individual teachers, including the SENCO and TAs.

These case studies do not represent an exhaustive list – either of the range of special educational needs or of the strategies that may work for children. They are intended to offer starting points for ideas for teachers and TAs to consider and try, and then develop after evaluating their impact on the children's progress.

Kuli, Year 8 – hearing impairment

Kuli has significant hearing loss. He has some hearing in his right ear but is heavily reliant on his hearing aid and visual cues, ranging from lip reading to studying body language and facial expression, to get the gist and tone of what people are saying. He often misses crucial details. Reading is a useful alternative input and his mechanical reading skills are good, but he does not always get the full message because of language delay. He has problems with new vocabulary and with asking and responding to questions.

Now in Year 8, he follows the same timetable as the rest of his class for most of the week but he has some individual tutorial sessions with a teacher of the deaf to help with his understanding of the curriculum and to focus on his speech and language development. This is essential but it does mean that he misses some classes, so he is not always up to speed with a subject.

He has a good sense of humour but appreciates visual jokes more than ones which are language based. He is very literal and is puzzled by all sorts of idioms. He was shocked when he heard that someone had been 'painting the town red' as he thought this was an act of vandalism! Even when he knows what he wants to say, he does not always have the words or structures to communicate accurately what he knows.

Everyone is very pleasant and quite friendly to him but he is not really part of any group and quite often misunderstands what other kids are saying. He has a learning assistant, which, again, marks him out as different. He gets quite frustrated because he always has ideas that are too complex for his expressive ability. He can be very sulky and has temper tantrums.

You will need to find out

The extent of Kuli's hearing loss, and how he can take part in discussion

Kuli may have a radio-mike system that connects directly to his hearing aid, and so he may have some access to the class discussion. Usually, the teacher would wear the microphone around the neck. However, if pupils contribute good ideas to share, it may be appropriate that the teacher allows the child to speak through the microphone so that Kuli is fully included. Clearly, this may slow down the pace of the lesson, and such discussions will have to be managed carefully, but Kuli's needs may have a beneficial effect on the classroom culture, because there will be a genuine and clear need for turn-taking, and allowing others to speak clearly.

Alternatively, Kuli may take enough information from a combination of lip reading and his hearing aid. This will necessitate a change in the classroom layout when discussions take place – perhaps a circular layout so that everyone can see each other when speaking.

Find time to listen carefully to Kuli, to understand how he enunciates words. This will be essential when, in whole-group settings, you ask him to contribute ideas.

You should consider

How to overcome the problem of Kuli's restricted access to handling mathematical vocabulary

The development of Kuli's use of mathematical vocabulary will be central to his overall progress in mathematics. It will not be picked up incidentally. The strategies below should help.

Planning with the TA

All of the following strategies should be discussed with the TA, including the TA's role with the whole class, rather than just with Kuli. It is worth being aware that having a TA constantly at his side may have the effect of *excluding* Kuli from the general run of the class, and a TA's support is in addition to the interactions Kuli will have with the teacher, not a substitute for them. To compensate for the extra attention Kuli may need in order to communicate with the teacher, the TA can be used to monitor the progress of other pupils in the class.

Some strategies you/the TA could try

Developing vocabulary

- When planning key questions for lessons – or more likely a series of lessons – especially those questions that are to be discussed as a whole class, they could be written (or typed) beforehand, so that Kuli can consider his responses carefully.
- Prepare vocabulary lists for lessons, to which the teacher, TA and the children can refer during any conversations. These will act as a visual prompt for the whole class, as well as giving Kuli a clearer idea of what is being discussed.
- The same vocabulary lists should be shared with Kuli and the TA beforehand, so that they can prepare for lessons together, if such time is available. Again, this practice could involve the whole class – the plenary session for one lesson could be used as a vocabulary preparation for the following lesson.

Using alternative learning media

Written questions can be translated into algebraic, visual or physical forms. This is not just a question of access, but also develops greater insight into the mathematics. For example, the question 'What two numbers have a sum of 9 and a product of 20?' could also be represented as:

$$a + b = 9, \qquad ab = 20, \qquad a = ? \qquad b = ?$$

Here the question is represented algebraically; in so doing, this enables us to teach children how algebra is used to express unknowns, and how it can be derived from words.

Chapter 3 discusses the benefits of making use of various learning styles, and offers details of the use of number lines and other visual/physical techniques.

Plan with the TA how diagrams, algebra or physical resources might be used as alternative ways of expressing ideas, and prepare these in advance for Kuli to use in lessons. It is highly likely that this translation of ideas will benefit many more – if not all – children in the class.

Kuli's expressive language

If Kuli contributes to the class but has difficulty in finding words, indicate that it is valid for him to express himself through diagrams or algebra. You could try to model his responses via diagrams – an example of this is given in Chapter 3, when illustrating how a child calculates 8 × 7 (see Figure 3.5), and the teacher 'translates' the calculation onto a number line. Kuli may be able to use the board himself for this purpose.

Harry, Year 7 – specific learning difficulties

Harry is a very anxious little boy and although he has now started at secondary school, he still seems to be a 'little boy'. His parents have been very concerned about his slow progress in reading and writing and arranged for a dyslexia assessment when he was aged 8. They also employ a private tutor who comes to the house for two hours per week, and they spend time each evening and at weekends hearing him read and working on phonics with him.

Harry expresses himself well orally, using words which are very sophisticated and adult. His reading is improving (RA 8.4) but his handwriting and spelling are so poor that it is sometimes difficult to work out what he has written. He doesn't just confuse *b* and *d* but also *h* and *y*, *p* and *b*. Increasingly, he uses a small bank of words that he knows he can spell.

His parents want him to be withdrawn from French on the grounds that he has enough problems with English. The French teacher reports that Harry is doing well with his comprehension and spoken French and is one of the more able children in the class.

Some staff get exasperated with Harry as he is quite clumsy, seems to be in a dream half the time and cannot remember a simple sequence of instructions. He has difficulty telling left from right and so is often talking about the wrong diagram in a book or out of step in PE and sport. 'He's just not trying,' said one teacher, while others think he needs 'to grow up a bit'.

He is popular with the girls in his class and recently has made friends with some of the boys in the choir. Music is Harry's great passion but his parents are not willing for him to learn an instrument at the moment.

You will need to find out

Specific strengths and weaknesses, both in general and within mathematics

Harry's strengths are the foundations upon which we can build his self-esteem in this subject. He may demonstrate some written language difficulties and may not accurately read texts, instructions or graphs, charts and diagrams, and these difficulties will have an effect on his general mathematics capabilities. However, he may well have strengths in handling numbers and have sound mental calculation skills, and it is therefore essential to find out what he can do in each of the areas of mathematics – and to what extent his specific difficulties hinder his understanding of any of these areas.

Standard written testing and examination procedures will inhibit Harry's capacity to demonstrate how he understands his mathematics. Oral assessment of Harry's work is therefore crucial, though time consuming (an accommodation with the TA for this task would enable the TA to undertake the oral assessment or release time for the teacher to do so). Furthermore, if teachers rely on written standard test scores to organise sets, then care must be taken that Harry is not placed in a set that may be inappropriate for his mathematical development, as this will have a serious and unnecessary impact on both his progress and his self-esteem.

How does Harry express himself?

At some stage, Harry will have to demonstrate his understanding both orally and in written form. The mathematics classroom should not be excluded from any writing strategies that are developed for Harry. These are likely to encourage the drafting process for any extended writing tasks, and therefore should include the use of ICT. If Harry drafts his ideas directly using ICT and is then encouraged to reread and redraft, either with TA support or as part of a class exercise where children are recording their work in pairs or groups, then the quality of his reasoning and his use of mathematical vocabulary are enhanced alongside the development of his general understanding of language.

Recording his voice (video, dictaphone apps on smartphones or voice recognition software, etc.) may be an alternative, effective way for Harry to present his reasoning. He may also benefit from using software that produces diagrams and charts (spreadsheets, dynamic geometry software – see below).

You should consider

Harry's personal organisation

Teachers may be interpreting Harry's genuine difficulties with personal organisation as 'immaturity'. Being organised requires us to have a mental map of a sequence of instructions and an understanding of the consequences of our actions. Young children are inexperienced with the latter; children with specific learning difficulties may have genuine problems with both.

The way to approach calculations

It is useful to consider the sequence in which one should approach calculations. The National Numeracy Strategy, although dated, promoted the following sequence that remains valid:

1. Children should use mental strategies as a first resort. They should always ask 'Can I do this in my head?'
2. Children should be encouraged to *use jottings to support mental calculations*.
3. Progress from expanded written methods to more compact written methods as and when children's understanding allows.

Developing mental arithmetic skills does not imply rote learning, e.g. multiplication facts. Kay and Yeo (2003) argue that 'it is simply not productive or appropriate for dyslexic learners to be required to learn the times table facts using the traditional rote-learning methods'. There are many ways in which an understanding of the times tables can be built through examining the structure of the number system, and children should be invited to reason about multiplication facts by examining links, e.g. 'How does 4×6 compare to 2×6, or 9×7 compare to 10×7?'

Some strategies you/the TA could try

Discussion, whole-class structured lessons; group work

Opportunities must be created for Harry to develop his skills of reasoning through discussion and group work. In this way, we are using his strength in self-expression and his own self-esteem will be raised, for he will have many opportunities to shine and have his understanding recognised through a medium that does not disadvantage him.

Given Harry's difficulties with both the written word *and* sequences of instructions, it is important that regular techniques are built up in the mathematics classroom for ensuring that children are clear about what they have to do. For this reason, the structured mathematics lesson has many benefits, where objectives and outcomes are made clear through discussion and children feel free to ask questions to clarify instructions.

Paired or group working will also help Harry to become involved in tasks, since through tackling the task together children will be constantly revisiting the aims and the purpose of the task, and the sequence of instructions they have to follow will be regularly discussed. In this way, the chances of Harry 'losing his way' become minimised.

Our presentation

Work that we present to children should be clear and large enough to read comfortably. Work on the board should not be cluttered; use colours effectively to emphasise main points.

The use of key vocabulary lists, specific to the series of lessons (Chapter 2), would benefit Harry greatly – he would have a ready reference for any written or oral work.

Other ICT packages

A variety of software/websites/apps could also be used to encourage oral work, and an understanding of fundamental mathematical concepts.

Dynamic geometry software packages (e.g. Cabri, Geometer's Sketchpad) will provide valuable tools to help Harry overcome the physical constraints of his difficulty. He can set instructions, using properties of shapes, to create shapes and diagrams, and can explore properties such as symmetry or area quickly and without having to create lots of diagrams for himself. Similar benefits may be found through regular use of various websites (e.g. Mymaths) and apps (e.g. Doodlemaths, etc.). These will also develop Harry's reasoning skills, which will be essential for him to overcome some of his memory difficulties.

Megan, Year 10 – wheelchair user

Megan is very outgoing, loud and tough. Everybody knows when she is around! No one feels sorry for her – they wouldn't dare! Megan has spina bifida and needs a wheelchair and personal care as well as educational support. She has upset a number of the less experienced classroom assistants, who find her a real pain. Some of the teachers like her because she is very sparky. If she likes a subject, she works hard – or at least she did until this year.

Megan has to be up very early so that her parents can help get her ready for school before the bus comes at 7.50 a.m. She lives out of town and is one of the first to be picked up and one of the last to be dropped off so she has a longer school day than many of her classmates. Tiredness can be a problem as everything takes her so long to do and involves so much effort.

Now she is 15, she has started working towards her GCSEs and has the potential to get several good passes, particularly in maths and sciences. She is intelligent but is in danger of becoming disaffected because everything is so much harder for her than for other children. Recently she has lost her temper with a teacher, made cruel remarks to a very sensitive child and turned her wheelchair round so she sat with her back to a supply teacher. She has done no homework for the last few weeks, saying that she doesn't see the point as 'no-one takes a crip seriously'.

You will need to find out

Special arrangements for examinations

Consideration must be given at an early stage to the kind of support Megan may need for sitting her examinations. She may need extra time, but if she is expected to use a scribe or perhaps ICT (though this is not so likely for a mathematics exam), then the opportunities for these kinds of support must be built into the regular classroom practice, as well as for mock examinations. Megan should be invited to join in making these decisions about both support and special examination arrangements.

You should consider

Megan should be fully involved in decision-making

Any strategy for helping Megan must take account of raising her self-esteem. Her self-perception will be highly sensitive to the relationships she develops with everyone at school – teachers and TAs, pupils and other adults. It will also be affected by the extent to which she feels she has control or responsibility over her educational future. She must be fully involved in both decision-making and the formulation of strategies. For example, if she has difficulties in sustaining the effort for the full range of subjects but is keen to attain the highest grades for her GCSEs in certain areas, she should be invited to discuss the suitability of a reduced timetable. This would enable her to have time at school to develop her coursework or homework assignments.

Appropriate grouping, managing support

In mathematics, it is hoped that she will be placed in the appropriate academic group first, and then any possibility of support explored after that. Schools often will have large groups for the most able pupils: Megan may find herself in a top set GCSE Mathematics group, commonly with 30 or more pupils. This will present its own problems – physically accommodating this number of pupils in many classrooms is difficult enough, but care must be taken that Megan has access both to the room itself and within it, and that she is also able to make a reasonable choice of where she is comfortable within the room. All these 'little' decisions add up to having an impact on her self-perception.

It is also less likely that the top set GCSE Mathematics group will enjoy the benefit of a TA to support Megan. If there is a TA, care should be taken as to how this TA actually works with her, and to what extent the TA can support Megan's mathematical development. Megan may not feel comfortable with a TA next to her all lesson; however, if the TA feels unable to support others in the group, whose needs are more likely to be with the high-level mathematics, then the TA may be placed in a difficult situation.

Some strategies you/the TA could try

ICT

ICT can be used effectively to support Megan. Clearly, basic software can take some of the menial work out of calculations and drafting her work. Dynamic geometry software packages (e.g. Cabri, Geometer's Sketchpad) are valuable tools to help her overcome the physical constraints of her difficulty. She can set instructions, using properties of shapes, to create shapes and diagrams, and can explore properties such as symmetry or area quickly and without having to create lots of diagrams for herself. Websites (e.g. Mymaths) and apps (e.g. Doodlemaths) will also provide her with an environment to explore mathematics without the need for manipulatives.

Regular group work; differentiation by paired grouping

However, it is possible to consider physical support for Megan from another source. If the culture within the whole classroom is geared towards mutual support rather than individualised working, then Megan will have a much greater opportunity (as will all the pupils) of belonging to it. To develop this culture, activities designed for group work and discussion would enable the teacher to structure groups so that pupils help each other – both to understand the mathematics and with any physical support for drawing/writing that may be needed.

Megan could also be considered an 'expert' in some groupings, rather than just the person who needs some help – she may be chosen to work with others because she has a particular skill or understanding in a specific area of mathematics; note McNamara and Moreton's (1997) discussion of differentiation. The desks may need to be pushed together; the classroom may be a little noisier because children are talking about their mathematics rather than trying to solve problems in isolation, but children's handling of mathematical vocabulary, reasoning and problem-solving will all improve, and Megan will not have to feel different, because the whole class will be operating in a way that includes everyone.

Managing classroom discussion

There are more direct ways of raising self-esteem. Class discussions, where children are invited to explain their methods and reasoning (for instance in making calculations, or in representing or interpreting data), should be the norm. The teacher can then model these explanations on the board, and the class should be invited to compare and evaluate methods. This technique can help to overcome misconceptions, but if the classroom culture enables such open discussions to take place as part of general practice, then children develop a greater self-respect by realising that their ideas are acknowledged and respected by their peers.

The rules of this classroom apply to everyone (see the box 'A conjecturing atmosphere' in Chapter 2). It works because it enables everyone to learn, and to be free both to succeed and to make mistakes, without ridicule. Megan's outgoing nature can be both positive and negative in effect. She may be inclined to dominate the class and must be reminded why we take turns to listen to each other; she may find a great deal of support from this way of working, in that she will be ready to contribute and will be rewarded with regular, positive feedback for her ideas.

Formative, peer and self-assessment

Finally, this class should certainly be developing their experience of assessing their own work. Chapter 4 illustrates some techniques for self- and peer assessment. Lesson objectives could be taken from the course specification, and pupils should be given regular opportunities to express their views on their progress.

If Megan finds herself belonging to a community that takes the views of all its pupils seriously, then she will have no cause to suggest that she is excluded from this. The examples of the way we work can be made explicit – listening to her self-assessment; using her expertise to help others in groups; the classroom atmosphere that respects the views of every pupil, through examining pupils' methods and reasoning; and the decisions about her timetable and support that she has made.

Steven, Year 8 – emotional and behavioural difficulties

'Stevie' is a real charmer – sometimes! He is totally inconsistent: one day he is full of enthusiasm, the next day he is very tricky and needs to be kept on target. He thrives on attention. In primary school, he spent a lot of time sitting by the teacher's desk and seemed to enjoy feeling special. If he sat there, he would get on with his work, but then as soon as he moved to sit with his friends, he wanted to make sure he was the centre of attention.

Now in Year 8, Steven sometimes seems lazy – looking for the easy way out – but at other times he is quite dynamic and has lots of bright ideas. He can't work independently and has a very short attention span. No one has very high expectations of him and he is not about to prove them wrong.

Some of the children don't like him because he can be a bully, but really he is not nasty. He is a permanent lieutenant for some of the tougher boys and does things to win their approval.

He is a thief but mostly takes silly things, designed to annoy rather than for any monetary value. He was found with someone's library ticket and stole one shoe from the changing rooms during PE.

Since his mother began a relationship with a new partner, there has been a deterioration in behaviour and Steven has also been cautioned by police after stealing from a local DIY store. He has just been suspended for throwing a chair at a teacher, but staff suspect this was because he was on a dare. He certainly knows how to get attention.

You will need to find out

Steven's interests and ways of learning that have been successful in the past

Steven clearly has a need to be the centre of attention, but this can be used to the advantage of the classroom. In finding out about Steven's interests and past successes (as part of a process for the whole group), you can demonstrate that he belongs to an environment where all children's views and ways of learning are respected. These interests could then be used as contexts for mathematical problems, e.g. football could be used as the context for work on handling data, and music in developing an understanding of patterns (leading to algebra). Furthermore, the interests could be used as part of the social well-being of the class ('How did your team get on?'; 'Have you learned to play that tune on the guitar yet?'). These kinds of conversations need not be long but can demonstrate the teacher's genuine interest in the pupils, giving a welcoming feeling to the class.

Steven's attention is more likely to be held in lessons where the types of task reflect his preferences (e.g. using physical mathematical equipment, or an emphasis on visual displays). Such materials may be all it takes to retain his attention so that he is not triggered into distracting behaviour.

You should consider

Classroom culture

Although Steven's behaviour difficulties are more specific and possibly more extreme than those of others in the group, it is important to note that his poor behaviour is more likely to occur where there is general, low-level disruption in the class as a whole. For most pupils, classroom behaviour reflects the culture of the whole class: if they perceive that the usual practice is to undermine the lesson with disruptive, well-timed comments, then they will join in. Steven may initiate some of the problems because he may not have the necessary self-control, but you are far more likely to have successful lessons with him if he works in a classroom that is well managed, where the rules are clear for all and where the general atmosphere is one of purposeful activity.

Body language, position

Sit down when working with Steven. Working at the same eye level is perceived as non-threatening. Steven will also read your facial expressions and your use of language carefully, and it is essential that you notice these aspects of your own behaviour as they are happening.

Some strategies you/the TA could try

Plan for managing Steven's behaviour

In addition to planning the mathematics of the lesson, it is important to be prepared for dealing with any of the expected possible situations that may arise from Steven's behaviour. Prepare your own actions, how you will deal with a range of possible responses, and be clear about the school's structures for dealing with problems that can no longer reasonably be contained in the classroom.

Be calm

Steven's behaviour is not likely to be directed *at you*, but *from him*. There may appear to be no difference, but keeping the perspective that he does not intend to threaten may allow you to deal with issues objectively.

Be consistent

Mean what you say, do as you promise. Steven needs to trust the people who work with him, and we act as role models for positive behaviour.

Be clear

Explain Steven's choices for behaviour, and the consequences of those choices.

Build the working relationship; repair and rebuild

If you are able to support him in an extra-curricular activity – sport, drama or music workshop – the working relationship will have a chance to develop positively. A shared humour is also useful to encourage pupils to stay on task and work with you, rather than against you.

If things go wrong – and you are human too – it is important for Steven to realise that there is no grudge, and that you both have a way back to get the working relationship together again. Make an opportunity to see Steven at times outside the classroom and perhaps arrange a meeting at registration, or break/lunchtime, to discuss a problem in a calmer and less charged atmosphere. It is all too easy for the classroom to become an arena for conflict, so it is necessary to follow up issues away from it.

Create regular opportunities to praise

This can usually be achieved in the discussion episodes of the lesson – where carefully directed questions can lead to Steven giving answers that are useful for the class. These questions could be focused on the calculation methods that Steven uses, or on something that he has found in his work, or on an observation he has made. The TA could help the teacher identify aspects of his work worthy of praise. If appropriate, use the merit system that exists in the school to reward good work – whether oral or written contributions. However, the praise must be earned; Steven will realise if it is being offered too freely.

Structured, episodic mathematics lessons; use a range of resources

Thinking of a structure to the lesson that has a series of episodes can help pupils who have difficulties in sustaining concentration for long periods of time. Different activities, based on the same or linked objectives, enable children to gain different perspectives of the same ideas – developing their understanding further. Different presentations, especially using ICT, and interactive whiteboards can be powerful tools for focusing attention.

Maintain high expectations, demonstrate achievement through effective use of assessment

It is easy to fall into the trap of offering low-level, easy work that does not challenge pupils with behavioural difficulties, but this creates a negative cycle of low achievement and low self-esteem, leading to more poor behaviour. The work may appear to keep them quiet for a while, but they will know that they are not being challenged and will feel the school is not offering them something worthwhile.

Most children will respond positively when they recognise that they are achieving, and the use of formative assessment (Chapter 4), coupled with activities appropriate for the age group, will ensure that expectations are kept high.

Matthew, Year 9 – cognitive and learning difficulties

Matt is a very passive boy. He has no curiosity, no strong likes or dislikes. One teacher said, 'He's the sort of boy who says yes to everything to avoid further discussion but I sometimes wonder if he understands anything.'

Now in Year 9, he is quite a loner. He knows all the children and does not feel uncomfortable with them but is always on the margins. Often in class he sits and does nothing, just stares into space. He is no trouble and indeed if there is any kind of conflict, he absents himself or ignores it. No one knows very much about him as he never volunteers any information. In French, he once said that he had a dog, and one teacher has seen him on the local common with a terrier but no one is sure if it is his.

He does every piece of work as quickly as possible to get it over with. His work is messy and there is no substance to anything he does, which makes it hard for teachers to suggest a way forward or indeed to find anything to praise. Matthew often looks a bit grubby and is usually untidy. He can be quite clumsy and loses things regularly but does not bother to look for them. He does less than the minimum.

He is in a low set for maths but stays in the middle. He has problems with most humanities subjects because he has no empathy and no real sense of what is required. When the class went to visit a museum for their work on the Civil War, he was completely unmoved. To him, it was just another building and he could not really link it with the work they had done in history.

You will need to find out

Matthew's interests and ways of learning that have been successful in the past

Taking an interest in Matthew will at least give him an experience of being at the centre and help to develop his expressive skills, and then his own interests can be used as effective contexts for problem-solving, where this is appropriate. Discussion with parents should reveal what he does at home, and may lead to extending his home activities.

Ask Matthew about the type of work he likes to do; Matthew is more likely to respond to work if it is in a form that facilitates his learning. Activities could be designed accordingly, to enhance his motivation.

Diagnostic information about Matthew's mathematical capabilities

Identify Matthew's strengths and weaknesses in the various mathematical areas. It is likely that Matthew has:

- poor understanding of basic mathematical ideas, such as the mathematical meaning of 'difference' or operations like division;
- limited understanding of mathematical vocabulary;
- poor communication skills;
- problems with logical reasoning;
- difficulty with problem-solving – applying knowledge to new situations.

Wider learning difficulties

Find out information about Matthew's literacy (e.g. reading age, spelling age), internal examination performance and primary school scores.

You should consider

Additional difficulties

Matthew may also experience some specific learning difficulties, as exemplified by his poor personal organisation and the weak presentation of his work.

Matthew may in addition experience dyspraxia, which will have an effect on his motor and language skills, and he may, therefore, need specific support in handling mathematical equipment.

Matthew may also have problems with auditory or visual memory. This will mean that he forgets instructions and is off task quite regularly.

Matthew's self-esteem

This is not likely to be high. Matthew will be well aware of his difficulties, but his survival technique of avoiding the task will not contribute to any feelings of success. If his work is so limited that it is 'difficult to praise', then situations must be engineered where he does receive – and enjoy – praise. These situations are most likely to arise initially in the oral interactions he has with the teacher and TA, and later, when working relationships are established, with his peers.

Some strategies you/the TA could try

Develop Matthew's oral skills – reasoning, explaining, listening and working in groups

Matthew's greatest difficulties need to be addressed – how he communicates and relates to others, and his powers of reasoning are directly related. Individualised book work will not address these – setting up situations where groups or pairs work together on solving a problem will begin to tackle Matthew's social difficulties and help him to engage more effectively with the work. The group will have to be monitored by the TA or teacher and occasionally led by one of them to model the desired ways of working. If Matthew has problems with staying on task, it is more likely that this will be overcome when a group has been given a shared task, and there is regular reaffirmation of the task and his role in completing it.

In problem-solving activities, Matthew must be given opportunities to explain how he tackles calculations, and identify any patterns or observations he has made. These opportunities may arise in paired work, with a TA or with the whole group.

Lesson or topic vocabulary (a short list placed at the front of the class) will support Matthew's explanations. Refer to it regularly through the lessons, and invite children to use some of the words as they discuss their ideas.

Developing an understanding of mathematical processes; structuring writing

Some processes can be structured, e.g. a problem-solving process can be unpicked into simpler steps, guiding children through solving. Appendix 21 can be used both for structuring a way of working and as a writing frame for the work. The data handling process (see Chapter 2) can be structured for children in a similar way.

ICT

Matthew's self-esteem may be enhanced when he produces work of a reasonable quality; the use of ICT can help facilitate this process, i.e. allowing him to draft and re-edit. The drafting process takes some effort, which Matthew does not demonstrate, and so he will need regular monitoring, TA/teacher support or paired work to ensure that a task is completed.

Monitor Matthew's use of mathematical equipment carefully

If Matthew displays clumsiness, he will find great difficulties in handling precision mathematical equipment such as a protractor, pair of compasses, pencil and ruler. Other specialised equipment (Cuisenaire rods, interlocking cubes) may also present physical difficulties, leading to frustration if appropriate support is not given.

Structured lessons; oral and mental starters

Matthew will respond more effectively to lessons organised into shorter episodes, where the outcomes of the tasks are made explicit and are achievable. Lesson starters could be used as regular practice for calculation skills, developing vocabulary and working with units of measurement.

Bhavini, Year 9 – visual impairment

Bhavini has very little useful sight. She uses a stick to get around school and some of the other children make cruel comments about this which she finds very hurtful. She also wears glasses with thick lenses which she hates. On more than one occasion, she has been knocked over in the corridor but she insists that these incidents were accidents and that she is not being bullied. However, her sight is so poor that she may not recognise pupils who pick on her.

She has a certain amount of specialist equipment such as talking scales in food technology and a video magnifier for textbooks, but now in Year 9 she is always conscious of being different. Her classmates accept her but she is very cut off as she does not make eye contact or see well enough to find people she knows to sit with at break. She spends a lot of time hanging around the support area. Her form tutor has tried to get other children to take her under their wing or to escort her to Humanities, which is in another building, but this has bred resentment. She has friends outside school at the local Phab club (physically handicapped/able bodied) and has taken part in regional VI Athletics tournaments, although she opts out of sport at school if she can. Some of the teachers are concerned about health and safety issues, and there has been talk about her being withdrawn from science.

She has a reading age approximately three years behind her chronological age and spells phonetically. Many of the teaching strategies used to make learning more interesting tend to disadvantage her. The lively layout of her French book with cartoons and speech bubbles is a nightmare. Even if she has a page on her video magnifier or has a photocopy of the text enlarged, she cannot track which bit goes where. At the end of one term she turned up at the support base asking for some work to do because 'they're all watching videos'.

You will need to find out

School strategies for receiving and presenting visual information

The school may develop alternative strategies for presentation, e.g. through the use of audio, ICT or any other specialised equipment.

Bhavini's mathematical capabilities

Bhavini's reading difficulties are not severe but may have had an effect on her understanding of some mathematical language, and therefore her understanding of mathematical concepts – especially in data handling, geometry and measures, and in solving written problems.

Arrangements for moving about school

Bhavini may be given more time to move from one classroom to another, and may therefore leave classrooms early. Alternatively, a pupil in the class may have responsibility for helping her.

Appropriate lighting for Bhavini's working environment

Bhavini may be affected by bright lights, or by an environment that is too dark. It may be necessary for Bhavini to work in a particular area of a particular room and have most of her lessons there.

Printed text

From the SENCO, find out exactly what Bhavini *can* see, and how materials should be presented. For example, she may be able to read a certain sized print, and certain types of font are likely to be preferable, e.g. clear fonts such as Arial, with certain types of spacing, as shown in Figure 6.1.

Arial size 12 point, **Arial size 12 point bold**

Arial size 12 point, **Arial size 12 point bold, double spacing**

Arial size 16 point, **16 point bold**

Arial size 16 point, **16 point bold, double spacing**

Arial size 24 point, **24 point bold**

Figure 6.1 Illustrating different sizes of font

When printed text is used in lessons, ensure that she has her own specially printed copies of the relevant material, with text kept to a minimum, clear and uncluttered.

Colours

Find out if using colour could be a useful source of support for Bhavini. Colours can be used effectively to clarify or emphasise, with specific sections of text highlighted in advance, or indicating different parts of a diagram or angles on a drawing. This strategy has the aim of clarifying rather than 'making learning interesting'.

You should consider

Producing written work

Produce worksheets/text with Bhavini's preferred font, size and any colour requirements to be used in class and for homework.

Using a smartphone dictaphone app or voice recognition software may be an alternative, effective way for Bhavini to present her reasoning, and with software that produces diagrams and charts (spreadsheets, dynamic geometry software – see 'Harry' in this chapter) she will be able to produce good quality written reports. A group could complete these reports – other pupils could contribute by using the same software as Bhavini.

However, it is important to recognise our values here: to what extent is learning achieved primarily through written activities? Is there a need for much of the work to be written? Evidence for learning can be clearly demonstrated through actions, the spoken word and mathematical constructions. These are outlined in Chapter 3.

Group/paired work

Bhavini will benefit greatly from working in a classroom where group/paired work is a strength. If the whole class is used to this way of working, there will be regular changes to the structure of the groups, and clearly defined roles for each member of the group. As there is no indication that Bhavini has difficulties with mathematical concepts, she can be given opportunities to be the 'expert' in a particular aspect of mathematics, so that she may help others. In return, the work in presenting ideas or translating visual information into auditory information can be shared.

Lighting, positioning

Bhavini should work in an appropriately lit environment, and you should not stand in silhouette against the window or other backlit source when addressing her. Glare from whiteboards or interactive whiteboards must be addressed when selecting her place in the classroom.

Some strategies you/the TA could try

Questioning, discussion

Begin questions with Bhavini's name, so that you are sure you have her attention. Draw her attention carefully to any part of the board, display or poster that is being discussed. She may not notice slight facial or hand gestures, so instructions will need to be verbally clear.

Oral work

It is likely that Bhavini can contribute ably to any oral episode of structured mathematics lessons. Ensure that she has many opportunities to develop her understanding of mathematical concepts in this way, as the written form will inevitably be slower for her.

Personal organisation, easy access to mathematical equipment

It is important for Bhavini to organise herself so that she can easily find any books, rulers, pencils and pens that she brings to class. Alternatively, she may be helped with a personal tray or cupboard space in the classroom. Any mathematical equipment should be clearly labelled, so that she may get it for herself if possible, to encourage her own independence.

Use of mathematical tools and equipment with tactile qualities

Some mathematical materials hold value for visually impaired pupils, as they also have tactile qualities, for example:

- **Cuisenaire rods** – for comparison of lengths/numbers; factors, fractions, decimals, ratio, percentages and some work on algebra;
- **Numicon** – used in a similar way to Cuisenaire rods but can be recognised through touch;
- **interlocking cubes** – for work on areas and volumes; enlargement of shapes, algebra (forming patterns and sequences). Large cubes are also available;
- **shape-building materials** (e.g. Geostrips) – for identifying and creating shapes and exploring their properties;
- **ATM mats** – tessellation, building regular solids, finding areas and perimeters of rectangles and squares;
- **Taktiles**, *Algebra through Geometry* (G. Giles/Tarquin) – to explore areas of shapes and express these areas algebraically;
- **probability equipment** – dice/coins/shakers with numbered counters – to explore experimental probability and compare with theoretical probability. Again, large dice and counters are also available for this work;
- **Diene's blocks, place value (arrow) cards** – to explore place value in numbers. These have tactile qualities to reinforce ideas of place value.

Use of other mathematical tools and equipment

- Some tools will present their own difficulties. Protractors and rulers, measuring jugs and scales using small calibrations will be impossible for Bhavini to read.
- It may be possible for Bhavini to read rulers with 1 cm divisions, but not millimetre divisions. Her understanding of measuring length can be enhanced through approximating lengths, e.g. to the nearest cm, or she may be invited to estimate lengths to nearest millimetres, having her estimations confirmed by another pupil or TA.
- In the same way, she may be able to read a protractor marked at every 10°, and estimate angles in between.

- As a kinaesthetic activity, try having the class stand up and turn through certain angles or bearings (having found north first).

Changing the media for learning – kinaesthetic activities, auditory activities, visualisation tasks

Chapter 3 explores some of the activities that may be useful to consider. Developing Bhavini's skills at personal visualisation will also be useful, e.g. translating into pictures a text that is read to the class.

Susan, Year 10 – complex difficulties, autistic spectrum disorder

Susan is a tall, very attractive girl who has been variously labelled as having Asperger's and 'cocktail party syndrome'. She talks fluently but usually about something totally irrelevant. She is very charming and her language is sometimes quite sophisticated, but her ability to use language for school work in Year 10 operates at a much lower level. Her reading is excellent on some levels but she cannot draw inferences from the printed word. If you ask her questions about what she has read, she looks blank, echoes what you have said, looks puzzled or changes the subject – something she is very good at.

She finds relationships quite difficult. She is very popular, especially with the boys in her class. They think she is a laugh. There have been one or two problems with some of the boys in school. Her habit of standing too close to people and her over-familiarity have led to misunderstandings which have upset her. Her best friend Laura is very protective of her and tries to mother her, to the extent of doing some of her work for her so she won't get into trouble.

Her work is limited. In art all her pictures look the same – very small, cramped drawings – and she does not like to use paint because 'it's messy'. She finds it very hard to relate to the wider world and sees everything in terms of her own experience. The class has been studying *Macbeth* and she has not moved beyond saying, 'I don't believe in witches and ghosts.'

Some teachers think she is being wilfully stupid or not paying attention. She seems to be attention-seeking as she is very poor at turn-taking and shouts out in class if she thinks of something to say or wants to know how to spell a word. When she was younger, she used to retreat under the desk when she was upset and had to be coaxed out. She is still easily offended and cannot bear being teased. She has an answer for everything and while it may not be sensible or reasonable, there is an underlying logic.

You will need to find out

What does Susan understand in mathematics?

If Susan has some difficulty with drawing inferences from the written word or with interpreting text, then it is very likely she will have difficulties in solving word problems. She may be fluent in some mathematical skills, where she is competent with handling procedures to make calculations, but she may not know *when* to apply particular skills. Offering a range of contexts for similar problems, and then helping her to identify the similarities between the problems, will help her to apply her skills more effectively.

Understand how she relates to you

She may not offer eye contact – it should not be expected. Her ways of relating to you may appear odd, e.g. she may keep an inappropriate physical space or her conversation may not match either the topic or the audience.

How much does Susan need individual space in which to work?

Susan may need a quiet, undisturbed area in which to work. She may be more productive if she is allowed to work on her own. Of course, she will need to be supervised carefully and helped when required.

Find out if lighting or noise affect her, and modify the classroom accordingly.

You should consider

Understanding of mathematical language

Some children with autism (about 10%) have a special creative or mathematical skill, but many will display difficulties with social interaction, communication and the development of imagination. These difficulties will affect mathematical development – the language of mathematics is accurate and complex, and understanding specific vocabulary will present challenges, especially where mathematical words have different meanings in common usage, e.g. 'property', 'operation', 'net'. There may also be difficulties where related meanings are illustrated precisely but a small difference exists – such as where vertical and horizontal are perpendicular to each other, but not all perpendicular pairs of lines are vertical and horizontal.

Susan's need for routine

A clear timetable and regular areas for working need to be set out for Susan. It may also be useful for her to have clear, visual references – timetables and labels for materials will support her in the school.

This need will also be addressed through structuring the mathematics lessons carefully, and clarifying the objectives and outcomes required of her.

Some strategies you/the TA could try

Your approach to Susan

- Be calm, patient, adaptable.
- Be positive, and have high expectations.
- Refer to Susan directly, even when speaking to her as part of a group.
- Be explicit about positive social behaviour, e.g. taking turns, listening to others and responding to the views of other pupils.
- Offer clear guidance for behaviour, and when needed disapprove of the *behaviour* not Susan.
- Despite her difficulties with jokes or humour, try to build these into your relationship with her – often 'running' jokes can be understood.

Development of language

Susan will find a mathematics dictionary, or a glossary, very useful in helping her learn precise meanings for mathematical terms. Vocabulary lists – especially specific lesson vocabulary – will help Susan focus on key words being used in the lesson.

Writing frames, including structured 'problem-solving' frames (e.g. Appendix 21), will support both Susan's pattern of working and her use of language in explaining her thinking.

Working in groups/pairs; using a TA

Susan's popularity may have emerged from inappropriate behaviour, perhaps an unfortunate use of language or her lack of appreciation of personal space. It is possible that the boys who think she's a laugh may encourage her to entertain them in classroom group situations. Furthermore, her friend Laura appears over-protective, and her actions in completing work for Susan end up being unhelpful. In each of these situations, Susan is not in control of her part in these relationships but is becoming increasingly disempowered by them. As a result, it is essential to:

- choose pairings/groups carefully – Susan should have opportunities to work with pupils who will help her to stay focused on task, who can help her and whom she can help with her own mathematical abilities;
- give clear guidelines as to what is expected of any collaboration, including defining the roles of each member of the group;
- monitor the work of the group;
- ask the TA to work with the group, modelling the expected behaviour.

The TA could also help Susan by listening to her ideas and helping her modify them as a preparation for any class discussion on a particular topic. This process will help Susan to refine her statements, both orally and in writing if necessary. As a result, she will learn how to improve on the language she uses to express herself, and the extra stage of thinking will help her develop the quality of her ideas.

Jenny, Year 7 – Down's syndrome

Jenny is a very confident child who has been cherished and encouraged by her mother and older brothers and sisters. She is very assertive and is more than capable of dealing with spiteful comments ('I don't like it when you call me names. You're cruel and I hate you'), but this assertiveness can lead to obstinacy. She is prone to telling teachers that they are wrong!

She has average skills in reading and writing, but her work tends to be unimaginative and pedestrian. She enjoys biology but finds the rest of the science curriculum hard going. She has started to put on weight and tries to avoid PE. She has persuaded her mother to provide a note saying that she tires easily, but staff know that she is a bundle of energy and is an active member of an amateur theatre group which performs musicals. She has a good singing voice and enjoys dancing.

She went to a local nursery and primary school and fitted in well. She always had someone to sit next to and was invited to all the best birthday parties. Teachers and other parents frequently praised her and she felt special.

Now in secondary school, everything has changed. Some of her friends from primary school have made new friendships and don't want to spend so much time with her. She is very hurt by this and feels excluded. She is also struck by how glamorous some of the older girls look, and this has made her more self-conscious.

You will need to find out

- The views of parents and the child herself about what has been achieved and what are reasonable goals to aim for in the mathematics curriculum.

- Strategies being applied over the whole school, to ensure a consistent approach, in terms of managing behaviour as well as learning.
- How to listen to Jenny, if her pronunciation is not clear.
- The difference between 'can't do' and 'won't do'. Tasks will need to be carefully designed so that Jenny understands what to do – not too hard, too easy or too long.

You should consider

Some general characteristics associated with Down's syndrome have a specific bearing on the child's mathematical development, notably:

- difficulties with thinking and reasoning, and applying knowledge to new situations;
- sequencing difficulties.

These difficulties can have a severe effect on the child's understanding of number, even to the point of consistent one-to-one matching when counting. Jenny may therefore experience many difficulties with mathematical ideas. Lorenz (1998) conducted research involving 25 secondary-aged children with Down's syndrome in mainstream schools, the most able of whom were working at the old national curriculum level 3 throughout KS3 and KS4. Similar results were shown by Buckley and Bird (1993).

There are associated behaviour problems, including a resistance to cooperate or undertake a task. Behaviour can change with effective management, and poor behaviour should not be accepted. Again, this aspect should be discussed with Jenny and her parents.

Too much one-to-one support can be counter-productive; Jenny should be given opportunities to work with other pupils who can provide positive models of behaviour and working. It may therefore not be appropriate for Jenny to work in a group where behaviour is already a problem.

The teacher must ensure regular contact with Jenny, to determine progress and effective planning.

Some strategies you/the TA could try

Use mathematical equipment as the basis for activities

Use a range of mathematical equipment to develop visual imagery to reinforce mathematical ideas, encourage reasoning from concrete situations and to promote discussion:

- **Cuisenaire rods** – for comparison of lengths/numbers; factors, fractions, decimals, ratio, percentages and some work on algebra;
- **Numicon** – used in a similar way to Cuisenaire rods but can be recognised through touch;
- **interlocking cubes** – for work on areas and volumes; enlargement of shapes, algebra (forming patterns and sequences);
- **shape-building materials** (Geostrips, Polydron) – for identifying and creating shapes and exploring their properties;
- **ATM mats** – tessellation, building regular solids, finding areas and perimeters of rectangles and squares;
- **Taktiles**, *Algebra through Geometry* (G. Giles/Tarquin) – to explore areas of shapes and express these areas algebraically;
- **probability equipment** – dice/coins/shakers with numbered counters – to explore experimental probability and compare with theoretical probability;
- **Diene's blocks, place value (arrow) cards** – to explore place value in numbers.

Note, however, that Jenny may have difficulties with her motor skills, and some frustrations may occur when using these materials. Always monitor her progress in this respect carefully.

Use Jenny's visual strengths

Visual resources, such as number lines, counting sticks and mind maps/spider diagrams (Chapter 3), can help the child in counting (forwards and backwards) and to develop an understanding of addition and subtraction.

Group/pair effectively

Establish a pattern of group or paired activities, to develop oral skills and cooperation. It may be useful to consider paired work with a child of weaker literacy skills, so that the partnership is mutually supportive, and so that Jenny can be the expert in reporting findings and expressing ideas. Many children with Down's syndrome experience poor auditory memory, and verbal instructions may quickly be forgotten. Working in groups can help overcome this difficulty, but it may also be helpful to have instructions written clearly as a reminder.

Questioning and instructions

Always allow good time for a response to questions. Develop vocabulary carefully, reinforcing familiar terms regularly. The use of lesson vocabulary lists (Chapter 2) will help with this.

Instructions should be kept short and simple, and tasks should be repeated regularly so that the child can use the techniques in increasingly varied situations.

Appendix 1 SEND legislation and guidance

The Children and Families Act: a different landscape

The Children and Families Act 2014 introduced radical changes to the requirements placed on both schools and teachers regarding the education and inclusion of pupils with special educational needs and disabilities. The first major revision of the SEND framework for 30 years, it introduced a new system to help children with special educational needs and disabilities and shaped how education, health and social care professionals should work in partnership with children, young people and their families.

The reforms introduced a system to support children and young people from birth up to the age of 25, designed to ensure smooth transitions across all services as they move from school into further education, training and employment. The reforms give particular emphasis to preparing children and young people for adulthood from the earliest years. This means enabling children to be involved at as young an age as possible in all decisions relating to their learning, therapy, medical treatment and support from social care. The result of this preparation should be that when young people reach the age of 16, they are able to be full and active participants in all important decisions about their life.

> There is now an important distinction made between a child and a young person. The Act gives significant new rights directly to young people when they are over compulsory school age but under the age of 25. Under the Act, a child becomes a young person after the last day of summer term during the academic year in which he or she turns 16. This is subject to a young person 'having capacity' to take a decision under the Mental Capacity Act 2005.

Throughout this book the term 'pupils with special educational needs and disabilities (SEND)' is used. A pupil has special educational needs if he or she:

- has a significantly greater difficulty in learning than the majority of others of the same age; or
- has a disability which prevents or hinders him or her from making use of facilities of a kind generally provided for others of the same age in mainstream schools or mainstream post-16 institutions.

(SEND Code of Practice 2015)

Section 19 principles

Central to Part 3 of the Children and Families Act 2014 is Section 19. This section emphasises the role to be played by parents/carers and young people themselves in all decision-making about their SEND provision.

Part C of Section 19 issues a new challenge to schools in that there is a clear expectation not only that parents and pupils will be invited to participate but also that they should be supported to do so. This will certainly involve the provision of relevant information to parents but schools could also consider providing other forms of support: both practical support, such as helping with translation services, or even transport to attend important meetings, and emotional support, such as advocacy or pre-meetings to prepare parents and pupils to take a full part in all decisions. Many parents will need only a minimal level of additional support, but others – especially those often portrayed as 'hard to reach' – may require considerably more.

Key questions:

- Do you know the wishes and feelings about education of your pupils with SEND and their parents? If not, how can you find out?
- What could you and others in your subject/departmental team do to integrate this information into your planning for and delivery of teaching and learning?
- What more could you do to reach out to parents who may be anxious about or unwilling to engage with school?

The SEND Code of Practice

As the quotation at the start of Chapter 1 makes clear, SEND provision is provision that is additional to or different from the high-quality, differentiated teaching to which all pupils are entitled. A school's first response to a pupil falling behind his or her peers should be to evaluate the quality of teaching and learning the pupil currently receives in all subjects. The pupil should be identified as having SEND only when the school is confident that all teaching is differentiated appropriately to meet that individual pupil's needs.

Once a pupil is identified as having SEND, schools are required to do whatever they can to remove any barriers to learning and to put in place effective provision, or 'SEND support'. This support must enable pupils with SEND to achieve the best possible outcomes.

Most schools and academies welcome pupils with a range of vulnerabilities, including special educational needs and disabilities, but may hesitate about including those with significant or complex needs. The reasons behind this reluctance are often a lack of expertise in an area of need, worries about behaviour and, most commonly expressed, concerns about the impact of that pupil's needs on the education of others.

The SEND Code of Practice is very clear that where the parent of a pupil with an education, health and care plan (EHC plan) makes a request for a particular school, the local authority *must* comply with that preference and name the school in the plan unless:

- it would be unsuitable for the age, ability, aptitude or SEN of the child or young person, or
- the attendance of the child or young person there would be incompatible with the efficient education of others, or the efficient use of resources.

(DfE 2015, 9.79, p. 172)

Legally, schools cannot refuse to admit a pupil who does not have an EHC plan because they do not feel able to cater for his or her needs, or because the pupil does not have an EHC plan.

Outcomes

Outcomes are written from the perspective of the pupil and should identify what the provision is intended to achieve. For example, do you think the following is an outcome for a pupil in Year 7 with literacy difficulties?

> For the next 10 weeks Jake will work on an online literacy program for 20 minutes three times each week.

It may be specific and measurable; it is achievable and realistic; and it is time targeted, so it is 'SMART' but it isn't an 'outcome'. What is described here is provision, i.e. the intervention that the school will use to help Jake to make accelerated progress.

Outcomes are intended to look forward to the end of the next stage or phase of education, usually two or three years hence. Teachers will, of course, set short-term targets covering between six and twelve weeks, and education and health plans will also include interim objectives to be discussed at annual reviews. So, what would be an outcome for Jake?

> By the end of Year 9, Jake will be able to read and understand the text-books for his chosen GCSE courses.

The online literacy course would then form a part of the package of provision to enable Jake to achieve this outcome.

The graduated approach

The SEND Code of Practice describes SEND support as a cyclical process of assess, plan, do and review that is known as the 'graduated approach'. This cycle is already commonly used in schools, and for pupils with SEND it is intended to be much more than a token, in-house process. Rather it should be a powerful mechanism for reflection and evaluation of the impact of SEND provision. Through the four-part cycle, decisions and actions are revisited, refined and revised. This then leads to a deeper understanding of an individual pupil's needs whilst also offering an insight into the effectiveness of the school's overall provision for pupils with SEND. The graduated approach offers the school, the pupil and his or her parents a growing understanding of needs and of what provision the pupil requires to enable him or her to make good progress and secure good outcomes. Through successive cycles, the graduated approach draws on increasingly specialist expertise, assessments and approaches, and more frequent reviews. This structured process gives teachers the information they need to match specific, evidence-based interventions to pupils' individual needs.

Evidence-based interventions

In recent years, a number of universities and other research organisations have produced evidence about the efficacy of a range of different interventions for vulnerable pupils and pupils with SEND. Most notable among this research is that sponsored by the Education Endowment Fund that offers schools valid data on the impact of interventions and the optimal conditions for their use. Other important sources of information about evidence based interventions for specific areas of need are the Communication Trust 'What Works?' website and 'Interventions for Literacy' from the SpLD/Dyslexia Trust. Both sites offer transparent and clear information for professionals and parents to support joint decisions about provision.

The Equality Act 2010

Sitting alongside the Children and Families Act 2014, the requirements of the Equality Act 2010 remain firmly in place. This is especially important because many children and young people who have SEND may also have a disability under the Equality Act. The definition of disability in the Equality Act is that the child or young person has 'a physical or mental impairment which has a long-term and substantial adverse effect on a person's ability to carry out normal day-to-day activities'.

'Long-term' is defined as lasting or being likely to last for 'a year or more', and 'substantial' is defined as 'more than minor or trivial'. The definition includes sensory impairments such as those affecting sight or hearing, and, just as crucially for schools, children with long-term health conditions such as asthma, diabetes, epilepsy and cancer.

As the SEND Code of Practice (DfE 2015, p. 16) states, the definition for disability provides a relatively low threshold, and includes many more children than schools may realise. Children and young people with some conditions do not necessarily have SEND, but there is often a significant overlap between disabled children and young people and those with SEND. Where a disabled child or young person requires special educational provision, they will also be covered by the SEND duties.

The Equality Act applies to all schools including academies and free schools, university technical colleges and studio schools, and also further education colleges and sixth form colleges – even where the school or college has no disabled pupils currently on roll. This is because the duties under the Equality Act are anticipatory in that they cover not only current pupils but also prospective ones. The expectation is that all schools will be reviewing accessibility continually and making reasonable adjustments in order to improve access for disabled pupils. When thinking about disabled access, the first thing that school leaders usually consider is physical access, such as wheelchair access, lifts and ramps. But physical access is only part of the requirement of the Equality Act and often is the simplest to improve. Your school's accessibility plan for disabled pupils must address all of three elements of planned improvements in access:

1. physical improvements to increase access to education and associated services;
2. improvements in access to the curriculum;
3. improvements in the provision of information for disabled pupils in a range of formats.

Improvements in access to the curriculum are often a harder nut to crack as they involve all departments and all teachers looking closely at their teaching and learning strategies and evaluating how effectively these meet the needs of disabled pupils. Often, relatively minor amendments to the curriculum or teaching approaches can lead to major improvements in access for disabled pupils, and these often have a positive impact on the education of all pupils. For example, one school installed a Soundfield amplification system in a number of classrooms because a pupil with a hearing loss had joined the school. The following year, the cohort of Year 7 pupils had particularly poor speaking and listening skills and it was noticed that they were more engaged in learning when they were taught in the rooms with the Soundfield system. This led to improvements in progress for the whole cohort and significantly reduced the level of disruption and off-task behaviours in those classes.

Schools also have wider duties under the Equality Act to prevent discrimination, to promote equality of opportunity, and to foster good relations. These duties should inform all aspects of school improvement planning from curriculum design through to anti-bullying policies and practice.

Significantly, a pupil's underachievement or behaviour difficulties might relate to an underlying physical or mental impairment which could be covered by the Equality Act. Each pupil is different and will respond to situations in his or her unique way so a disability should be considered in the context of the child as an individual. The 'social model' of disability sees the environment as the primary disabling factor, as opposed to the 'medical model' that focuses on the individual child's needs and difficulties. School activities and environments should be considered in the light of possible barriers to learning or participation.

Appendix 2 Departmental policy

Whether the practice in your school is to have separate SEND policies for each department or to embed the information on SEND in your whole-school inclusion or teaching and learning policies, the processes and information detailed below will still be relevant.

Good practice for pupils with SEND is good practice for all pupils, especially those who are 'vulnerable' to underachievement. Vulnerable groups may include looked-after children (LAC), pupils for whom English is an additional language (EAL), pupils from minority ethnic groups, young carers, and pupils known to be eligible for free school meals/Pupil Premium funding. Be especially aware of those pupils with SEND who face one or more additional vulnerabilities and for whom effective support might need to go beyond help in the classroom.

It is crucial that your departmental or faculty policy describes a strategy for meeting pupils' special educational needs within your particular curricular area. The policy should set the scene for any visitor, from supply staff to inspectors, and make a valuable contribution to the department handbook. The process of developing a departmental SEND policy offers the opportunity to clarify and evaluate current thinking and practice within the maths team and to establish a consistent approach.

The SEND policy for your department is a significant document in terms of the leadership and management of your subject. The preparation and review of the policy should be led by a senior manager within the team because that person needs to have sufficient status to be able to influence subsequent practice and training across the department.

What should a departmental policy contain?

The starting points for your departmental SEND policy will be the whole-school SEND policy and the SEND Information Report that, under the Children and

Families Act 2014, all schools are required to publish. Each subject department's own policy should then 'flesh out' the detail in a way that describes how things will work in practice. Writing the policy needs to be much more than a paper exercise completed merely to satisfy the senior management team and Ofsted inspectors. Rather, it is an opportunity for your staff to come together as a team to create a framework for teaching maths in a way that makes your subject accessible, not only to pupils with special educational needs and disabilities but to all pupils in the school. It is also an ideal opportunity to discuss the impact of grouping on academic and social outcomes for pupils. Bear in mind that the Code of Practice includes a specific duty that 'schools must ensure that pupils with SEND engage in the activities of the school alongside pupils who do not have SEND' (6.2, p. 92).

We need to be careful in maths that, when grouping pupils, we are not bound solely by measures in reading and writing, but also take into account reasoning and oral language abilities. It is vital that social issues are also considered if pupils are to be able to learn effectively. Having a complement of pupils with good oral ability will lift the attitude and attainment of everybody within a group.

Who should be involved in developing your SEND policy?

The job of developing and reviewing your policy will be easier if tackled as a joint endeavour. Involve people who will be able to offer support and guidance such as:

- the school SEND governor;
- the SENCO or other school leader with responsibility for SEND;
- your support staff, including teaching assistants and technicians;
- the school data manager, who will be able to offer information about the attainment and progress of different groups;
- outside experts from your local authority, academy chain or other schools;
- parents of pupils with SEND;
- pupils themselves – both with and without SEND.

Bringing together a range of views and information will enable you to develop a policy that is compliant with the letter *and* principle of the legislation, that is relevant to the context of your school, and that is useful in guiding practice and improving outcomes for all pupils.

The role of parents in developing your departmental SEND policy

As outlined in Appendix 1, Section 19 of the Children and Families Act 2014 raises the bar of expectations about how parents should be involved in and influence the work of schools. Not only is it best practice to involve parents of pupils with SEND in the development of policy, but it will also help in 'getting it right' for both pupils and staff. There are a number of ways, both formal and informal, to find out the views of parents to inform policy writing, including:

- a focus group;
- a coffee morning/drop-in;
- a questionnaire/online survey;
- a phone survey of a sample of parents.

Parents will often respond more readily if the request for feedback or the invitation to attend a meeting comes from their son or daughter.

Where to start when writing a policy

An audit can act as a starting point for reviewing current policy on SEND or writing a new policy. This will involve gathering information and reviewing current practice with regard to pupils with SEND, and is best completed by the whole department, preferably with some input from the SENCO or another member of staff with responsibility for SEND within the school. An audit carried out by the whole department provides a valuable opportunity for professional development so long as it is seen as an exercise in sharing good practice and encourages joint planning. It may also facilitate your department's contribution to the school provision map. But, before embarking on an audit, it is worth investing some time in a departmental meeting, or ideally a training day, to raise awareness of the legislation around special educational needs and disabilities and to establish a shared philosophy across your department.

The following headings may be useful when you are establishing your departmental policy:

General statement of compliance

- What is the overarching aim of the policy? What outcomes do you want to achieve for pupils with SEND?
- How are you complying with legislation and guidance?
- What does the school SEND Information Report say about teaching and learning and provision for pupils with SEND?

Example

All members of the department will ensure that the needs of all pupils with SEND are met, according to the aims of the school and its SEND policy . . .

Definition of SEND

- What does SEND mean?
- What are the areas of need and the categories used in the Code of Practice?
- Are there any special implications for your subject area?

(See Chapter 1.)

Provision for staff within the department

- Who has responsibility for SEND within the department?
- What are the responsibilities of this role? E.g.

  - liaison between the department and the SENCO;
  - monitoring the progress of and outcomes for pupils with SEND, e.g. identifying attainment gaps between pupils with SEND and their peers;
  - attending any liaison meetings and providing feedback to colleagues;
  - attending and contributing to training;
  - maintaining departmental SEND information and records;
  - representing the needs of pupils with SEND at departmental level;
  - liaising with parents of pupils with SEND;
  - gathering feedback from pupils with SEND on the impact of teaching and support strategies on their learning and well-being.

(The post can be seen as a valuable development opportunity for staff, and the name of this person should be included in the policy. However, where responsibility for SEND is given to a relatively junior member of the team, there must be support and supervision from the head of the department to ensure that the needs of pupils with SEND have sufficient prominence in both policy and practice.)

- What information about pupils' SEND is held, where is it stored and how is it shared?
- How can staff access additional resources, information and training?
- How will staff ensure effective planning and communication between teachers and teaching assistants?
- What assessments are available for teachers in your department to support accurate identification of SEND?

> **Example**
>
> The member of staff with responsibility for overseeing the provision of SEND within the department will attend liaison meetings and subsequently give feedback to the other members of the department. S/he will maintain the department's SEND file, attend and/or organise appropriate training and disseminate this to all departmental staff. All information will be treated with confidentiality.

Provision for pupils with SEND

- How are pupils' special educational needs identified? E.g.

    - observation in lessons;
    - assessment of class work/homework;
    - end of module tests/progress checks;
    - annual examinations/SATs/GCSEs;
    - reports.

- How is progress measured for pupils with SEND?
- How do members of the department contribute to individual learning plans, meetings with parents and reviews?
- What criteria are used for organising teaching groups?
- How/when can pupils move between groups?
- What adjustments are made for pupils with special educational needs and/ or disabilities in lessons and homework?
- How do we use information about pupils' abilities in reading, writing, speaking and listening when planning lessons and homework?
- What alternative courses are available for pupils with SEND?
- What special arrangements are made for internal and external examinations?
- What guidance is available for working effectively with support staff?

Here is a good place also to put a statement about the school behaviour policy and any rewards and sanctions, and how the department will make any necessary adjustments to meet the needs of pupils with SEND.

> **Example**
>
> The staff in the maths department will aim to support pupils with SEND to achieve the best possible outcomes. They will do this by supporting pupils to achieve their individual targets as specified in their individual learning plans, and will provide feedback for progress reviews. Pupils with SEND will be included in the departmental monitoring system used for all pupils.

Resources and learning materials

- Is any specialist equipment used in the department?
- How are differentiated resources developed? What criteria do we use (e.g. literacy levels)?
- Where are resources stored and are they accessible for both staff and pupils?

> **Example**
>
> The department will provide suitably differentiated materials and, where appropriate, specialist resources to meet the needs of pupils with SEND. Alternative courses and examinations will be made available where appropriate for individual pupils. Support staff will be provided with curriculum information in advance of lessons and will be involved in lesson planning. A list of resources is available in the department handbook.

Staff qualifications and continuing professional development (CPD)

- What qualifications and experience do the members of the department have?
- What training has already taken place, and when? What impact did that training have on teaching and learning, and progress for pupils with SEND?
- How is training planned? What criteria are used to identify training needs?
- What account of SEND is taken when new training opportunities are proposed?
- Is a record kept of training completed and ongoing training needs?

> **Example**
>
> A record of training undertaken, specialist skills and training required will be kept in the department handbook. Requests for training will be considered in line with the department and school improvement plan.

Monitoring and reviewing the policy

- How will the policy be monitored?
- Who will lead the monitoring?
- When will the policy be reviewed?

> **Example**
>
> The departmental SEND policy will be monitored by the head of department on a planned annual basis, with advice being sought from the SENCO as part of the three-yearly review process.

Conclusion

Creating a departmental SEND policy should be a developmental activity that will improve teaching and learning for all pupils, but especially for those who are vulnerable to underachievement. The policy should be a working document that will evolve and change over time; it is there to challenge current practice and to encourage improvement for both pupils and staff. If departmental staff work together to create the policy, they will have ownership of it; it will have true meaning and be effective in clarifying good practice.

An example of a departmental policy for you to amend is available on the website: www.routledge.com/9781138283404.

Appendix 3 Types of SEND

Introduction

This appendix is a starting point for information on the special educational needs most frequently encountered in mainstream schools. It describes the main characteristics of each area of special educational need and disability (SEND) with practical ideas for use in subject areas, and contacts for further information.

There is a measure of repetition, as some strategies prove to be effective with a whole range of pupils (and often with those who have no identified SEND). However, the layout enables readers an 'at a glance' reminder of effective approaches and facilitates copying for colleagues and TAs.

The SEND Code of Practice (DfE 2015) outlines four broad areas of need. These are:

- communication and interaction;
- cognition and learning;
- social, emotional and mental health difficulties;
- sensory and/or physical needs.

These broad areas are not exclusive and pupils may have needs that cut across some or all of them. Equally, pupils' difficulties and needs will change over time. The terms used in this chapter are helpful when reviewing and monitoring special educational provision, but pupils' individual talents and interests are just as important as their disability or special educational need. Because of this, specific terms or labels need to be used with care in discussion with parents, pupils or other professionals. Unless a pupil has a firm diagnosis, and parents and pupil understand the implications of that diagnosis, it is more appropriate to describe the features of the special educational need rather than use the label. For example, a teacher might describe a pupil's spelling difficulties but not use the term 'dyslexic'.

There is a continuum of need within each of the special educational needs and disabilities listed here. Some pupils will be affected more than others and show fewer or more of the characteristics described.

Pupils with other, less common special educational needs may be included in some schools, and additional information on these conditions may be found in a variety of sources. These include the school SENCO, local authority support services, educational psychologists and online information, for example on the Nasen SEND Gateway and disability charity websites such as those of Mencap, CAF or I CAN, the children's communication charity.

Further information

www.nasen.org.uk
www.mencap.org.uk
www.cafamily.org.uk
www.ican.org.uk

Attention deficit disorder (with or without hyperactivity) ADD/ADHD

Attention deficit hyperactivity disorder is one of the most common childhood disorders and can continue through adolescence and adulthood. ADHD can occur in pupils of any intellectual ability and may also cause additional problems, such as sleep and anxiety disorders. The features of ADHD usually diminish with age, but many individuals who are diagnosed with the condition at a young age will continue to experience problems in adulthood.

Main characteristics

- short attention span or easily distracted by noise and movement
- difficulty in following instructions and completing tasks
- difficulty in listening to and processing verbal instructions
- restlessness, inability to keep still causing frequent fidgeting
- difficulty with moderating behaviour such as constant talking, interrupting and calling out
- difficulty in waiting or taking turns
- impulsivity – acting without thinking about consequences

How can the maths teacher help?

- Make eye contact and use the pupil's name when speaking to him.
- Keep instructions simple – the one sentence rule.
- Provide clear written instructions.
- Position the pupil away from obvious distractions, e.g. windows, computer screens.
- Provide clear routines and rules, and rehearse them regularly.
- Encourage the pupil to repeat instructions (to you or the TA) before starting work.
- Tell the pupil when to begin a task.
- Give two choices – avoid the option of the pupil saying 'no', e.g. 'Do you want to write in blue or black pen?'
- Give advanced warning when something is about to happen. Signal a change or finish with a time, e.g. 'In two minutes I need you (pupil name) to . . .'
- Give specific praise – catch him being good, give attention for positive behaviour.
- Give the pupil responsibilities so that others can see him in a positive light and he develops a positive self-image.

Further information

ADDISS	020 8952 2800	www.addiss.co.uk
ADHD Foundation	0151 237 2661	www.adhdfoundation.org.uk
Young Minds	020 7089 5050	www.youngminds.org.uk
Autism (ASD)		

Asperger syndrome

Asperger syndrome is a type of autism. People with Asperger syndrome do not have 'learning difficulties' as such, but they do have difficulties associated with being on the autistic spectrum. They often want to make friends but do not understand the complex rules of social interaction. They may have impaired fine and gross motor skills, with writing being a particular problem. Boys are more likely to be affected - with the ratio being 10:1 boys to girls. Because they appear 'odd' and naive, these pupils are particularly vulnerable to bullying.

Main characteristics

- **Social interaction**
  Pupils with Asperger syndrome want friends but have not developed the strategies necessary for making and sustaining meaningful friendships. They find it very difficult to learn social norms and to pick up on social cues. Social situations, such as assemblies and less formal lessons, can cause great anxiety.

- **Social communication**
  Pupils have appropriate spoken language but tend to sound formal and pedantic, using limited expression and possibly an unusual tone of voice. They have difficulty using and understanding non-verbal language such as facial expression, gesture, body language and eye contact. They may have a literal understanding of language and do not grasp implied meanings.

- **Social imagination**
  Pupils with Asperger syndrome need structured environments, and to have routines they understand and can anticipate. They may excel at learning facts but have difficulty understanding abstract concepts and in generalising information and skills. They often have all-consuming special interests.

How can the maths teacher help?

- Liaise with parents, especially over homework.
- Create as calm a classroom environment as possible.
- Allow to sit in the same place for each lesson.
- Set up a 'work buddy' system for your lessons.
- Provide additional visual cues in class, such as visual timetables and task activity lists.
- Give the pupil time to process questions and respond.
- Make sure pupils understand what you expect of them.
- Offer alternatives to handwriting for recording work.
- Prepare pupils for changes to routines well in advance.

- Give written homework instructions.
- Have your own class rules and apply them consistently.

Further information

www.autism.org.uk/about/what-is/asperger.aspx

Autism spectrum disorder (ASD)

Autism is a developmental disability that affects how a person communicates with, and relates to, other people. It also affects how they make sense of the world around them. It is often referred to as a spectrum or ASD which means that, while all people with autism share certain difficulties, the condition may affect them in different ways. Pupils with ASD cover the full range of academic ability and the severity of the disability varies widely. Some pupils also have learning disabilities or other difficulties, such as dyslexia. Four times as many boys as girls are diagnosed with an ASD.

Main characteristics

- **Social interaction**
  Pupils with ASD find it difficult to understand social behaviour and this affects their ability to interact with others. They do not always understand social contexts. They may experience high levels of stress and anxiety in settings that do not meet their needs or when routines are changed. This can lead to inappropriate behaviour.

- **Social communication**
  Understanding and use of non-verbal and verbal communication are impaired. Pupils with an ASD have difficulty understanding the communication of others and in developing effective communication themselves. They may have a literal understanding of language. Many are delayed in learning to speak, and some people with ASD never develop speech at all.

- **Social imagination and flexibility of thought**
  Pupils with an ASD have difficulty in thinking and behaving flexibly which may result in restricted, obsessional or repetitive activities. They are often more interested in objects than people, and have intense interests in such things as trains and vacuum cleaners. Pupils work best when they have a routine. Unexpected changes in those routines will cause distress.

Some pupils with autistic spectrum disorders have a different perception of sounds, sights, smell, touch and taste, and this can affect their response to these sensations.

How can the maths teacher help?

- Collaborate with parents (perhaps via the SENCO) as they will have many useful strategies.
- Provide visual supports in class: objects, pictures, a symbol timetable, etc.
- Always consider potential sensory issues.

- Give advance warning of any changes to usual routines.
- Provide either an individual desk or the opportunity to work with a buddy.
- Take into account the pupil's individual learning preferences, e.g. by allowing for a choice of output for a task, a digital recording, a short video, a drawing, a photograph with caption, a word-processed document, an e-book, a mini-book.
- Give individual instructions using the pupil's name at the beginning of the request, e.g. 'Paul, bring me your book.'
- Be alert to pupils' levels of anxiety.
- Develop social interactions using a buddy system or Circle of Friends.
- Avoid using metaphor, idiom or sarcasm – say what you mean in simple language.
- Use pupils' special interests as motivations.
- Help pupils to manage potentially difficult situations by rehearsing them beforehand (perhaps with a TA) or through the use of social stories.

Further information

The National Autistic Society	020 7833 2299	www.autism.org.uk
Autism Education Trust	0207 903 3650	www.autismeducationtrust.org.uk

Cerebral palsy (CP)

Cerebral palsy is a condition that affects muscle control and movement. It is usually caused by an injury to the brain before, during or after birth. Pupils with cerebral palsy have difficulties in controlling their muscles and movements as they grow and develop. Problems vary from slight clumsiness to more severe lack of control of movements. Pupils with CP may also have learning difficulties. They may use a wheelchair or other mobility aid.

Main characteristics

There are three main forms of cerebral palsy:

- *spastic cerebral palsy* – associated with stiff or tight muscle tone, resulting in a decreased range of movement; this stiffening of muscle tone can be very painful and affect different parts of the body
- *dyskenetic cerebral palsy* – sustained or intermittent involuntary muscle contractions often affecting the whole body
- *ataxic cerebral palsy* – an inability to activate the correct pattern of muscles during movement, resulting in an unsteady gait with balance difficulties and poor spatial awareness

Pupils with CP may also have communication difficulties.

How can the maths teacher help?

- Gather information from parents and therapists involved with the pupil (perhaps via the SENCO until parents' evening provides an opportunity for a face-to-face chat).
- Consider the classroom layout to maximise access.
- Have high academic expectations.
- Use visual supports: objects, pictures, symbols.
- Arrange for a work or subject buddy.
- Speak directly to the pupil rather than through a teaching assistant.
- Ensure access to appropriate ICT equipment and check that it is used effectively.
- Consider late arrival to and early exit from lessons to avoid potential problems in crowded corridors.

Further information

Scope   0808 800 3333   www.scope.org.uk

Down's syndrome

Down's syndrome (DS) is the most common identifiable cause of learning disability. This is a genetic condition caused by the presence of an extra chromosome 21. People with DS have varying degrees of learning difficulties ranging from mild to severe. They have a specific learning profile with characteristic strengths and weaknesses. All share certain physical characteristics but will also inherit family traits, in physical features and personality. They may have additional sight, hearing, respiratory and heart problems.

Main characteristics

- delayed motor skills
- taking longer to learn and consolidate new skills
- limited concentration
- difficulties with generalisation, thinking and reasoning
- sequencing difficulties
- stronger visual than aural skills
- better social than academic skills

How can the maths teacher help?

- Ensure that the pupil can see and hear you and other pupils.
- Speak directly to the pupil and reinforce speech with facial expression, pictures and objects.
- Use simple, familiar language in short sentences.
- Check instructions have been understood.
- Give the pupil time to process information and formulate a response.
- Break lessons up into a series of shorter, varied and achievable tasks.
- Accept alternative ways of responding to tasks: drawings, audio or video recordings, symbols, etc.
- Set individual tasks linked to the work of the rest of the class.
- Provide age-appropriate resources and activities.
- Allow the pupil to work with more able peers to give good models of work and behaviour.
- Provide a work buddy.
- Expect pupil to work unsupported for part of every lesson to avoid over-dependence on adult support.

Further information

| Down's Syndrome Association | 020 8682400 | www.downs-syndrome.org.uk |

Foetal alcohol syndrome

Foetal alcohol syndrome (FAS) or foetal alcohol spectrum disorders (FASD) are umbrella terms for diagnoses relating to a child's exposure to alcohol before birth. Alcohol can affect the development of all cells and organs, but it is the brain and nervous system that are particularly vulnerable. Each person with FAS/D may face a range of difficulties across a spectrum from mild to severe.

Main characteristics

- visual impairment
- sleep problems
- speech and language delay
- impulsivity and/or hyperactivity
- memory problems
- inappropriate social behaviour

How can the maths teacher help?

- Gather information from parents and other professionals involved with the pupil to find the most effective ways of teaching him/her (perhaps through the SENCO in the first instance).
- Find out the pupil's strengths and use these as starting points for learning.
- Keep instructions simple and offer information in verbal and visual form, supported by mime, gesture and facial expression.
- Ensure class routines are explicit and followed consistently.
- Use concrete and positive language, e.g. 'Walk' rather than 'Don't run'.
- Check the pupil knows and understands any school or class rules.
- Specify clearly what is expected for any task or activity.
- Provide a memory mat or audio recording facilities to support retention of information, e.g. homework tasks, spellings, etc.

Further information

www.drinkaware.co.uk/fas

Learning disability (learning difficulty)

The terms 'learning disability' and 'learning difficulty' are used to describe a wide continuum of difficulties ranging from moderate (MLD) to profound and multiple (PMLD). Pupils with learning disabilities find it harder to understand, learn and remember new things, meaning they may have problems across a range of areas such as communication, being aware of risks or managing everyday tasks.

Moderate learning difficulties (MLD)

The term 'moderate learning difficulties' is used to describe pupils who find it extremely difficult to achieve expected levels of attainment across the curriculum, even with a well-differentiated and flexible approach to teaching. These pupils do not find learning easy and can suffer from low self-esteem and sometimes exhibit unacceptable behaviour as a way of avoiding failure. For all pupils with learning disabilities, the social aspect of school is a crucial element in their development and understanding of the 'culture' of young people, so it is important for them to have friends who don't have learning disabilities as well as those who do. As the SEND Code of Practice says at 6.2 (p. 92): 'Schools must . . . ensure that children and young people with SEN engage in the activities of the school alongside pupils who do not have SEN.'

Main characteristics

- difficulties with reading, writing and comprehension
- problems understanding and retaining mathematical skills and concepts
- immature social and emotional skills
- limited vocabulary and communication skills
- short attention span
- underdeveloped coordination skills
- inability to transfer and apply skills to different situations
- difficulty remembering what has been taught previously
- difficulty with personal organisation such as following a timetable, remembering books and equipment

How can the maths teacher help?

- Find out about the pupil's strengths, interests and areas of weakness.
- Have high expectations.
- Establish a routine within your lessons.
- Keep tasks short and varied.
- Keep listening tasks short or broken up with other activities.
- Provide word lists, writing frames and shortened versions of text to be read.

- Offer alternative methods of recording information, e.g. drawings, charts, labelling, diagrams, use of tachnology.
- Check previously gained knowledge and build on this (it may be at a very different level from that of other pupils in the class).
- Offer instructions and information in different ways, e.g. use a cartoon avatar with voice-over to introduce the lesson (see www.voki.com) or an electronic poster to present information (see www.glogster.com).
- Be explicit about the expected outcome; demonstrate or show examples of completed work. WAGOLL it! (What a Good One Looks Like)
- Use practical, concrete, visual examples to illustrate explanations.
- Question the pupil to check he has grasped a concept or has understood instructions.
- Make sure the pupil always has something to do.
- Use lots of praise, instant rewards, catch them trying hard. (Beware of praising the effort and not the outcome – the emphasis should be on praising the effort, strategies, focus, perseverance and information-seeking in relation to the outcome, with particular emphasis on learning and progress.)

Severe learning difficulties (SLD)

This term covers a wide and varied group of pupils who have significant intellectual or cognitive impairments. Many have communication difficulties and/or sensory impairments in addition to more general learning difficulties. Some pupils may also have difficulties in mobility, coordination and perception, and the use of signs and symbols will be helpful to support their communication and understanding. Pupils' academic attainment will also vary, with many able to access a well-differentiated mainstream curriculum and achieve at GCSE level.

How can the maths teacher help?

- Liaise with parents (perhaps through the SENCO in the first instance).
- Arrange a work/subject buddy.
- Use visual supports: objects, pictures, symbols.
- Allow time for pupils to process information and formulate responses.
- Set differentiated tasks linked to the work of the rest of the class.
- Set achievable targets for each lesson or module of work.
- Accept different recording methods: drawings, audio or video recordings, photographs, etc.
- Give access to computers where appropriate.
- Plan a series of short, varied activities within each lesson.

Profound and multiple learning difficulties (PMLD)

Pupils with profound and multiple learning difficulties have complex learning needs. In addition to severe learning difficulties, pupils have other significant difficulties, such as physical disabilities, sensory impairments or severe medical conditions. Pupils with PMLD require a high level of adult support, both for their learning needs and for personal care.

Pupils with PMLD are able to access the curriculum largely through sensory experiences. Some pupils communicate by gesture, eye pointing or symbols, others by very simple language. The concept of progress for pupils with PMLD covers more than academic attainment. Indeed, for some pupils who may have associated medical conditions, simply maintaining knowledge and skills will count as good progress.

How can the maths teacher help?

- Work closely with teaching/support assistants working with the pupil.
- Consider the classroom layout so that wheelchairs can move around easily and safely.
- Identify all possible sensory opportunities in your lessons.
- Use additional sensory supports: objects, pictures, music, textures, etc.
- Use photographs to record the pupil's experiences and responses.
- Set up a work/subject buddy rota for the class.
- Identify opportunities for the pupil to work in groups.

Further information

Mencap	020 7454 0454	www.mencap.org.uk
Foundation for People with Learning Disabilities	020 7803 1100	www.learningdisabilities.org.uk

Physical disability (PD)

There is a wide range of physical disabilities, and pupils with PD span all academic abilities. Some pupils are able to access the curriculum and learn effectively without additional educational provision. They have a disability but do not have a special educational need. For other pupils, the impact of their disability on their education may be significant, and the school will need to make adjustments to enable access to the curriculum.

Some pupils with a physical disability have associated medical conditions that may have an impact on their mobility. These conditions include cerebral palsy, heart disease, spina bifida and muscular dystrophy. They may also have sensory impairments, neurological problems or learning disabilities. They may use a wheelchair and/or additional mobility aids. Some pupils will be mobile but may have significant fine motor difficulties that require support or specialist resources. Others may need augmentative or alternative communication aids.

Pupils with a physical disability may need to miss lessons to attend physio-therapy or medical appointments. They are also likely to become very tired as they expend greater effort to complete everyday tasks. Teachers need to be flexible and sensitive to individual pupil needs.

How can the maths teacher help?

- Get to know the pupil (and parents) so that they will help you make the right adjustments.
- Maintain high expectations.
- Consider the classroom layout.
- Give permission for the pupil to leave lessons a few minutes early to avoid busy corridors and give time to get to the next lesson.
- Set homework earlier in the lesson so instructions are not missed.
- Speak directly to the pupil rather than through a teaching assistant.
- Let pupils make their own decisions.
- Ensure access to appropriate ICT equipment for the lesson – and check that it is used.
- Offer alternative ways of recording work.
- Plan to cover work missed through illness or medical appointments.
- Be sensitive to fatigue, especially towards the end of the school day.

Further information

Scope   0808 800 3333   www.scope.org.uk

Social, emotional and mental health difficulties

This area includes pupils who experience a wide range of difficulties characterised in a number of ways, including becoming withdrawn or exhibiting behavioural difficulties. Behaviours such as these may reflect underlying mental health difficulties including depression, anxiety and eating disorders. These difficulties can be seen across the whole ability range and have a continuum of severity. Attachment disorders and attention deficit disorder will also be part of this continuum. Pupils with special educational needs in this area are those who have persistent difficulties despite the school having in place an effective school behaviour policy and a robust personal and social curriculum.

Main characteristics

- inattentive, poor concentration and lacking interest in school and school work
- easily frustrated and anxious about changes
- difficulty working in groups
- unable to work independently, constantly seeking help or attention
- confrontational: verbally aggressive towards pupils and/or adults
- physically aggressive towards pupils and/or adults
- destroys property: their own and that of others
- appears withdrawn, distressed, unhappy or sulky, and may self-harm
- lacks confidence and self-esteem
- may find it difficult to communicate
- finds it difficult to accept praise

How can the maths teacher help?

- Check the ability level of the pupil and adapt expectations of work accordingly.
- Consider the pupil's strengths and interests and use these as motivators.
- Tell the pupil clearly what you expect in advance, for work and for behaviour.
- Talk to the pupil to find out more about them and how they feel about learning.
- Focus your comments on the behaviour not on the pupil ('That was a rude thing to say' rather than 'You are a rude boy').
- Use positive language and gestures and verbal praise whenever possible.
- Tell the pupil what you want them to do: 'I need you to . . .', 'I want you to . . .', rather than asking, 'Will you . . .?'; this avoids confrontation and the possibility that there is room for negotiation.
- Give the pupil a choice between two options.
- Stick to what you say. Be consistent.
- Give the pupil class responsibilities to increase self-esteem and confidence.
- Plan a 'time out' system; ask a colleague for help with this.

Further information

SEBDA   01233 622958   www.sebda.org

Sensory impairments

Hearing impairment (HI)

The term 'hearing impairment' is a generic term used to describe all hearing loss. The main types of loss are monaural, conductive, sensory and mixed loss. The degree of hearing loss is described as mild, moderate, severe or profound.

How can the maths teacher help?

- Find out about the degree of the pupil's hearing loss and the likely implications for your lessons.
- Allocate the most appropriate seating position for the pupil (e g. away from the hum of computers, with the better ear facing towards the speaker).
- Check that the pupil can see your face for facial expressions and lip reading.
- Make sure the light falls on your face and lips. Do not stand with your back to a window.
- Provide a list of vocabulary, context and visual clues, especially for new subjects.
- During class discussion, allow one pupil to speak at a time and indicate where the speaker is.
- Check that any aids are working.
- If you use interactive whiteboards, ensure that the beam does not prevent the pupil from seeing your face.

Further information

| Action on Hearing Loss | 020 7296 8000 | www.actiononhearingloss.org.uk |
| The National Deaf Children's Society | 020 7490 8656 | www.ndcs.org.uk |

Visual impairment (VI)

Visual impairment refers to a range of difficulties and includes the disabilities of those pupils with monocular vision (vision in one eye), those who are partially sighted and those who are blind. Pupils with visual impairment cover the whole ability range and some pupils may have additional special educational needs.

How can the maths teacher help?

- Check the optimum position for the pupil, e.g. for a monocular pupil their good eye should be towards the action.

- If you move around the classroom, give the pupil an aural cue as to where you are, e.g. by snapping your fingers or using a clicker before you speak.
- Always provide the pupil with his own copy of any texts, with enlarged print where possible.
- Check the accessibility of ICT systems (enlarged icons, screen readers, etc.)
- Do not stand with your back to the window as this creates a silhouette and makes it harder for the pupil to see you.
- Draw the pupil's attention to displays – which they may not notice.
- Make sure the floor is kept free of clutter.
- Let the pupil know if there is a change to the layout of a space.
- Ask if there is any specialist equipment that the pupil requires for your subject, such as enlarged print dictionaries or additional lighting.

Further information

Royal National   0303 123 9999   www.rnib.org.uk
Institute for Blind
People (RNIB)

Multi-sensory impairment (MSI)

Pupils with multi-sensory impairment have a combination of visual and hearing difficulties. They may also have other disabilities that make their situation complex. A pupil with these difficulties is likely to need a high level of individual support.

How can the maths teacher help?

- Liaise with specialist teachers and support staff to ascertain the appropriate provision within your subject.
- Learn how to use alternative means of communication, as appropriate.
- Be prepared to be flexible and to adapt tasks, targets and assessment procedures.

Specific learning difficulties (SpLD)

The term 'specific learning difficulties' includes dyslexia, dyscalculia and dyspraxia.

Dyslexia

The term 'dyslexia' is used to describe difficulties that affect the ability to learn to read, write and/or spell stemming from a difficulty in processing the sounds in words. Although found across a whole range of ability, pupils with dyslexia often have strengths in reasoning and in visual and creative skills, but their particular difficulties can result in underachievement in school. While pupils can learn strategies to manage the effects of dyslexia, it is a life-long condition and its effects may be amplified at times of stress or in unfamiliar situations.

Main characteristics of dyslexia

- The pupil may frequently lose his place while reading, make errors with even high-frequency words and have difficulty reading names, blending sounds and segmenting words. Reading and writing require a great deal of effort and concentration.
- Written work may seem messy, with uneven letters and crossings out. Similarly shaped letters may be confused, such as b/d/p/q, m/w, n/u, 6/9, and letters in words may be jumbled, such as tired/tried. Spelling difficulties often persist into adult life and these pupils can become reluctant writers.
- Personal organisation can be underdeveloped.

How can the maths teacher help?

- Be aware of the pupil's individual strengths and areas of difficulty – speak to him directly to identify effective support strategies.
- Teach and encourage the use of ICT, where appropriate.
- Make sure pupils have the 'big picture' for the lesson/topic.
- Provide word lists and photocopies rather than expect the pupil to copy from the board.
- Colour-code word lists to aid memory.
- Link words and phrases to physical movements.
- Provide support in reading word problems.
- Allow extra time for tasks, including assessments and examinations.
- Support the pupil in recording homework to be completed – and time scales.

Further information

www.dyslexiaaction.org.uk

Dyscalculia

The term 'dyscalculia' is used to describe difficulties in processing number concepts and mastering basic numeracy skills. These difficulties might be in marked contrast to the pupil's developmental level and general ability in other areas.

Main characteristics

- The pupil may have difficulty counting by rote, writing or reading numbers, miss out or reverse numbers, have difficulty with mental maths, and be unable to remember concepts, rules and formulae.
- In maths-based concepts, the pupil may have difficulty with money, telling the time, giving/following directions, using right and left and sequencing events. He may also be prone to losing track of turn-taking, e.g. in team games or dance.
- Poor time management and organisation skills.

How can the maths teacher help?

- Make full use of ICT to support learning.
- Encourage the use of rough paper for drafting.
- Check understanding at regular intervals.
- Offer a framework for setting out work.
- Provide concrete, practical tasks that are appropriate for the pupil's age.
- Allow extra time for tasks, including assessments and examinations.

> **Further information**
>
> www.bdadyslexia.org.uk/dyslexic/dyscalculia

Dyspraxia

Dyspraxia is a common developmental disorder that affects fine and gross motor coordination and may also affect speech. The pattern of coordination difficulties will vary from person to person and will affect participation and functioning in everyday life as well as in school.

Main characteristics of dyspraxia

- difficulty in coordinating movements, making pupils appear clumsy and possibly leading to difficulty with using geometry equipment
- difficulty with handwriting and drawing

- confusion between left and right
- difficulty following sequences and multiple instructions
- weak grasp of spatial concepts (in, above, behind, etc.)
- may misinterpret situations, take things literally
- limited social skills, resulting in frustration and irritability
- possible articulation difficulties

How can the maths teacher help?

- Be sensitive to the pupil's limitations in games and practical/outdoor activities and plan tasks to enable success.
- Limit the amount of writing expected.
- Ask the pupil questions to check his understanding of instructions/tasks.
- Use concrete objects to model prepositions, e.g. an object on/in/under/ behind a box.
- Pass a soft toy/ball around a circle or get pupils to nominate who is to answer the next question rather than throw the object, or use a random name generator like the one found on the classtools.net website, or the 'Decide now' app.
- Check the pupil's seating position to encourage good presentation (both feet resting on the floor, desk at elbow height and ideally with a sloping surface on which to work).

Further information

Dyspraxia Foundation   01462 455 016   www.dyspraxiafoundation.org.uk

Speech, language and communication difficulties (SLCD)

Pupils with speech, language and communication difficulties have problems that affect the full range of communication and the development of skills may be significantly delayed. Such difficulties are very common in young children but most problems are resolved during the primary years. Problems that persist beyond the transfer to secondary school will be more severe and will have a significant effect on self-esteem and personal and social relationships. The development of literacy skills is also likely to be affected. Even where pupils learn to decode, they may not understand what they have read. Sign language and symbols offer pupils an additional method of communication.

Pupils with speech, language and communication difficulties cover the whole range of academic abilities.

Main characteristics

- Speech difficulties: difficulties with expressive language may involve problems in articulation and the production of speech sounds, or in coordinating the muscles that control speech. Pupils may have a stammer or some other form of dysfluency.
- Language/communication difficulties: receptive language impairments lead to difficulty in understanding other people. Pupils may use words incorrectly with inappropriate grammatical patterns, have a reduced vocabulary, or find it hard to recall words and express ideas. Some pupils will also have difficulty using and understanding eye contact, facial expression, gesture and body language.

How can the maths teacher help?

- Gather information about the pupil (perhaps via the SENCO) and talk to the pupil himself about strategies to support him in your subject.
- Use visual supports such as objects, pictures, symbols.
- Use the pupil's name when addressing him to alert him to a question or instruction.
- Give one instruction at a time, using short sentences.
- Give pupils time to respond before repeating a question.
- Provide a good model of spoken language and rephrase pupil's response where appropriate: 'I think you are saying that . . .'
- Make sure pupils understand what they have to do before expecting them to start a task.
- Pair with a work/subject buddy.
- Give access to a computer or other ICT equipment appropriate to the subject.
- Give written homework instructions.

Further information

I CAN	0845 225 4073 or 020 7843 2552	www.ican.org.uk
AFASIC	0300 666 9410 (Helpline)	www.afasic.org.uk

Tourette's syndrome (TS)

Tourette's syndrome is a neurological disorder characterised by 'tics' – involuntary rapid or sudden movements or sounds that are frequently repeated. There is a wide range of severity of the condition, with some people having no need to seek medical help whilst others have a socially disabling condition. The tics can be suppressed for a short time but will be more noticeable when the pupil is anxious or excited.

Main characteristics

- *Physical tics* range from simple blinking or nodding through to more complex movements and conditions such as echopraxia (imitating actions seen) or copropraxia (repeatedly making obscene gestures).
- *Vocal tics* may be as simple as throat clearing or coughing but can progress to be as extreme as echolalia (the repetition of what was last heard) or coprolalia (the repetition of obscene words).

TS itself causes no behavioural or educational problems but pupils may also have other associated disorders such as attention deficit hyperactivity disorder (ADHD) or obsessive compulsive disorder (OCD).

How can the maths teacher help?

- Establish a good rapport with the pupil.
- Talk to the class about TS and establish an understanding and tolerant ethos.
- Agree an 'escape route' signal, should the tics become overwhelming for the pupil or disruptive for the rest of the class.
- Allow the pupil to sit at the back of the room to be less obvious.
- Give access to a computer to reduce the need for handwriting.
- Allow for non-verbal responses to questions, e.g. use of mini-whiteboards, sorting pictures into a correct sequence, simple puzzles such as Tarsia.
- Make sure the pupil is not teased or bullied.
- Be alert for signs of anxiety or depression.

Further information

Tourettes Action	UK 0300 777 8427 (Helpdesk)	www.tourettes-action.org.uk

Appendix 4 The front of the classroom

The number line

−10 −9 −8 −7 −6 −5 −4 −3 −2 −1 0 1 2 3 4 5 6 7 8 9 10

The whiteboards

Objectives	Lesson title	Date	Vocabulary

Appendix 5 Posters/displays for the classroom

Number lines – decimals, fractions and percentages

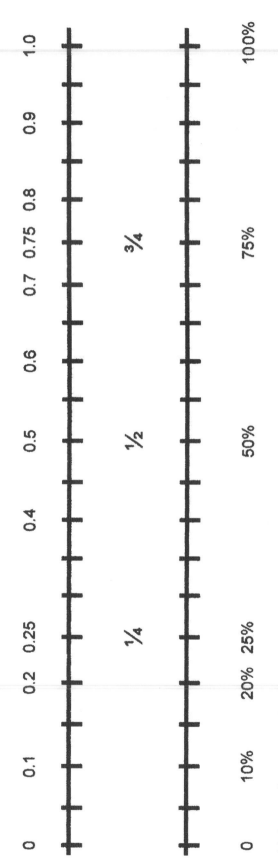

Using colour can highlight patterns. Not all the numbers should be inserted – this can be used as a teaching tool, for children to develop an understanding of the patterns and links in the number systems being used here. Children should be invited to predict other points on the number line (even beyond the 1.0 or 100% shown here) and justify and to check their predictions.

Appendix 6 Showing the links between place value column headings, powers, fractions, decimals and metric units

HTU – Place Value – Powers – Metric Units

M	HTh	TTh	Th	H	T	U	.	t	h	th	tth	hth	mth
Million	Hundred thousand	Ten thousand	Thousand	Hundred	Ten	Unit	point	Tenth	Hundredth	Thousandth	Ten thousandth	Hundred thousandth	Millionth
		$10\times10\times10$		10×10				$\frac{1}{10}$	$\frac{1}{10\times10}$				
			10^{3}							10^{-3}			
			1000				.	$1/10$	$1/100$				
			km			m	.		cm	mm			
						l	.		cl				
			kg			g				mg			

$\longrightarrow \div 10$

$\longrightarrow \times 10$

Can you complete the diagram? What links each row?

What is similar about the Thousand and the Thousandths columns? Are the same kinds of similarities in other pairs of columns?

If we divide or multiply by 10 to move to the next column, what do we multiply or divide by when moving across two columns? Three columns?

Appendix 7 Times table charts

Table	×1	×2	×3	×4	×5	×6	×7	×8	×9	×10	×	×	×

The above blank may be used in a number of ways, again to illustrate links and patterns to help children understand the number system, e.g.

Table	×1	×2	×3	×4	×5	×6	×7	×8	×9	×10	×	×	×
2	2	4	6		10		14						
0.2	0.2	0.4					1.4						
20	20	40			100								

Appendix 8 Further examples of making explicit links with number sequences

Table	×1	×2	×3	×4	×5	×6	×7	×8	×9	×10	×	×	×
¼	¼	½	¾	1									
½	½	1	1½	2	2½	3	3½						
¾	¾												

Table	×1	×2	×3	×4	×5	×6	×7	×8	×9	×10	×	×	×
2	2	4	6	8									
4	4	8	12	16									
8	8	16	24										

Appendix 9 100 squares

This presentation of the number square reflects the popular language of 'going up in tens' and of numbers getting bigger.

91	92	93	94	95	96	97	98	99	100
81	82	83	84	85	86	87	88	89	90
71	72	73	74	75	76	77	78	79	80
61	62	63	64	65	66	67	68	69	70
51	52	53	54	55	56	57	58	59	60
41	42	43	44	45	46	47	48	49	50
31	32	33	34	35	36	37	38	39	40
21	22	23	24	25	26	27	28	29	30
11	12	13	14	15	16	17	18	19	20
1	2	3	4	5	6	7	8	9	10

1	2	3	4	5	6	7	8	9	10
11	12	13	14	15	16	17	18	19	20
21	22	23	24	25	26	27	28	29	30
31	32	33	34	35	36	37	38	39	40
41	42	43	44	45	46	47	48	49	50
51	52	53	54	55	56	57	58	59	60
61	62	63	64	65	66	67	68	69	70
71	72	73	74	75	76	77	78	79	80
81	82	83	84	85	86	87	88	89	90
91	92	93	94	95	96	97	98	99	100

Appendix 10 Using the number line

For fractions of quantities:

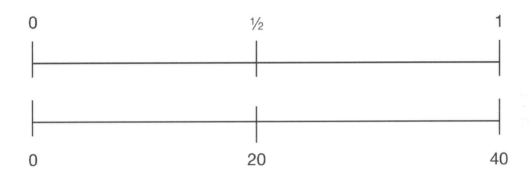

For comparing fractions, decimals and percentages:

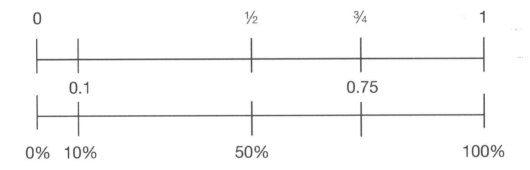

Appendix 11 Physical resources for the mathematics department

Number and calculations, including fractions, decimals and percentages

Many of these resources can also be used for work in algebra.

Equipment	Some possible uses
Counting stick	Number sequences, tables
Number lines	For all four operations
Arrow cards	Demonstrating place value
Interlocking cubes	Number sequences, leading to algebra
Diene's blocks	Place value, relating numbers and decimals
Cuisenaire rods	Factors, fractions, decimals, percentages; algebra
ATM Developing Number software	Place value, tables, complements
Target boards	Calculations
Calculators – all types, including scientific, graphic	Comparing calculators reveals the need for the order of operations; calculator skills need to be explicitly taught
ICT – spreadsheet	Extended calculations, presentation of data
Money	Money and decimals
Fraction tiles/poster	Comparing relative sizes and equivalence of fractions

Algebra (see also above – Cuisenaire rods, interlocking cubes, etc.)

Equipment	Some possible uses
Algebra through Geometry (G. Giles/Dime)	Expressing areas algebraically Collecting like terms
Graph drawing software	

Geometry and measures

Equipment	Some possible uses
ATM Shape Mats	Tessellations, geometric reasoning Making 3D shapes
Shape construction equipment (Polydron, Geostrips)	Construction, reasoning
Compasses, rulers, protractors, etc. There are also specialist resources for children with motor difficulties.	Construction, measurement
Paper – various mathematical papers	Construction, reasoning
Height measures – wall scales	
Dynamic geometry software (e.g. Cabri, Geometer's Sketchpad)	Reasoning
Interlocking cubes	Building shapes, exploring volume and surface area, enlargements
Small mirrors	Symmetry
Balance scales, weights and modelling clay	
Various jugs of different capacities	
Clocks and timetables	
Platonic solids pack	Recognising 3D shapes
A variety of very large 2D shapes (at least 30 cm high)	Hide and reveal activity, where part of the shape is hidden and gradually revealed as children try to identify the shape

Data handling and probability

Equipment	Some possible uses
Dice, coins	Probability
Probability pots (based on DIME probability kits)	Probability
Spreadsheet/database	Data handling

Other

Equipment	Some possible uses
Mini-whiteboards, pens and wipes	Rapid assessment of pupils' understanding
	Calculations, diagrams
Posters	In each of the topic areas, to support discussion
Games	Counting, recognising numbers on dice, probability, developing strategies, shape recognition, use of coordinate grids (e.g. Battleships)
	Calculations (e.g. 24 game)

Appendix 12 Sources list

Supplier	Contact	Resources
ATM	Tel: 01332 346 599 www.atm.org.uk	General maths resources including problem-solving activities and physical resources (e.g. MAT tiles, cubes, jigsaws, puzzles etc.)
BEAM	Tel: 02076 843 323 www.beam.co.uk	Physical maths resources including place value cards, customised dice, counters and various types of mathematical paper
Bowland Maths	Tel: N/A www.bowlandmaths.org.uk	Problem-solving activities
Chartwell-Yorke Ltd	Tel: 01204 811 001 www.chartwellyorke.com	Maths software and associated books, e.g. Cabri
Don Steward	Tel: N/A www.donsteward.blogspot.co.uk	Blog of ideas for teachers; problem-solving activities
Invicta Plastics Ltd	Tel: 0116 272 0555 www.invictaeducationshop.com	Geostrips – shape construction equipment
Learning Resources	Tel: 01553 762 276 www.learningresources.com	General maths resources, including manipulatives, games, etc.
The Mathematical Association	Tel: 0116 221 0013 www.m-a.org.uk	Books of ideas for teachers

Supplier	Contact	Resources
Mathsbox	Tel: 01773 825 835 www.mathsbox.org.uk	Website resources for teachers: treasure hunts, review activities, bingo, etc.
Mr Barton Maths	Tel: N/A www.mrbartonmaths.com	Website resources for teachers, students and parents
MyMaths	Tel: 01536 452 970 www.mymaths.co.uk	Online lessons and homework activities
NRICH	Tel: 01223 766 839 www.nrich.maths.org	Problem-solving activities
Polydron International Ltd	Tel: 01285 770 055 www.polydron.com	Shape construction equipment
Shell Centre	Tel: 0115 951 4410 www.mathshell.com	Mathematical publications including works on numeracy through problem-solving and patterns with problems and numbers
Tarquin Publications	Tel: 01379 384 218 www.tarquingroup.com	Physical maths resources including posters, books, games and textbooks

Appendix 13 Dotty activities

Resources – 3 × 3; 4 × 4; 5 × 5 squared dotty paper; full-page squared dotty paper, isometric dotty paper

1) Equivalent perimeters

Objectives: *Recognise perpendicular and parallel lines. Identify right angles.*

Find perimeters of shapes. Apply understanding of perimeter to reason about shapes.

Activity

What shapes can you draw on 4 × 4 dotty paper, using only perpendicular lines? Find the perimeters of your shapes.

Key questions

How many of them have a perimeter of 12 cm?

Why do the cross and the square (3 cm × 3 cm) have the same perimeter?

Which type of shape has a different perimeter?

Which shape has the largest perimeter?

What are the angles inside the shapes?

2) Square areas

Objectives: *Find areas of squares, by counting, and by geometric reasoning.*

Activity

Using 5 × 5 dotty paper, how many different squares can you draw?

(There are eight: four aligned vertically, four 'skewed'. Note that many children would wish to call the skewed squares diamonds. But they are still squares.)

Key questions

What are the areas of these squares?

What are the lengths of the sides of your squares?

Tabulate your results, showing side length and area.

The numbers 1, 4, 9, 16 are known as square numbers. Why? Why not the others?

Why can't you make an area of three squares on this paper?

3) Shapes on dotty paper

Objectives: *Make shapes with increasing accuracy; find reflective symmetry in regular polygons; classify quadrilaterals.*

Activity

On 4 × 4 dotty paper, can you draw all these?

a) Five different sized squares?
b) A rhombus (not a square)?
c) Nine different parallelograms?
d) How many different rectangles?
e) How many different kites?
f) How many different trapezia?
g) As many different isosceles triangles as you can.

Key questions

Can you show the lines of symmetry on these shapes?

Can you find the areas of each of these?

What makes a rhombus different from a parallelogram or from a square?

How many of these shapes could be drawn on 3 × 3 dotty paper?

Appendix 14 3 × 3 dotty paper

Appendix 15 4 × 4 dotty paper

Appendix 16 5 × 5 dotty paper

Appendix 17 A writing frame for a data handling task

My hypothesis is _____

_____

(Your hypothesis could begin with the words 'I believe that . . .' or 'My opinion
is that . . .')

Planning and data collection

To find out if my hypothesis is correct, I am going to collect some data. The
data I intend to collect is _____

_____

_____

_____

This is how I am going to collect my data: _____

_____

_____

_____

Presentation

To record my results, I am going to use _____

_____

_____

To present my results, I am going to use _____

_____

_____

because _____

_____

_____

_____

Calculations

I will need to make the following calculations: _____

_____

_____

_____

_____

_____

Conclusion

My hypothesis was true/false/not proven, because _____

_____

_____

_____

_____

_____

_____

_____

Evaluation

What further data should I collect? _____

_____

_____

_____

_____

_____

What other calculations could I make? _____

_____

_____

_____

_____

Were my presentations the most effective I could have chosen? _____

_____

_____

_____

_____

What others could I have used? _____

_____

_____

_____

Appendix 18 Questions in mathematics, using Bloom's taxonomy (1956)

Focus	Possible questions
Knowledge	What is the special name of this quadrilateral? What is the product of 8 × 6?
Comprehension	Explain how we calculate . . . Describe the shape in this picture.
Application	What shape of graph do you expect? Can you predict . . .
Analysis	Should the lines on this graph reach the axes? Can you break this problem down into smaller steps? What does this data tell us?
Synthesis	Can you find a rule for this generalisation? Can you predict the next number in the sequence? Can you predict the 10th number? What if we didn't have brackets in this calculation?
Evaluation	Which calculation method is better in this case? Is this data valid? Did you choose to collect the right data? What errors are there in this diagram/chart/graph?

Appendix 19 Interpreting graphs and charts in lesson starters

What is wrong?

Year	%
1999	0.1
2000	0.2
2001	0.25
2002	0.32
2003	0.38

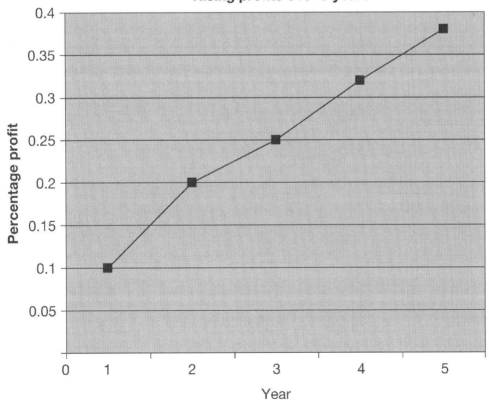

What is wrong?

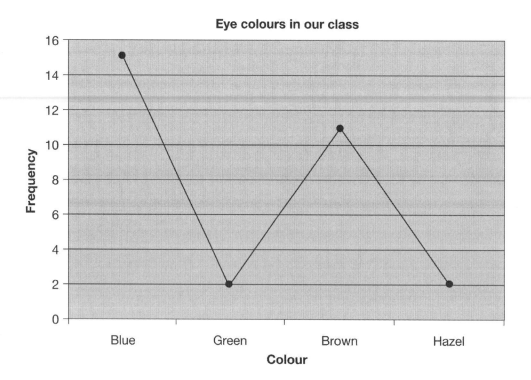

Appendix 20 Linking equations

Use the spider diagram to find links between equations.

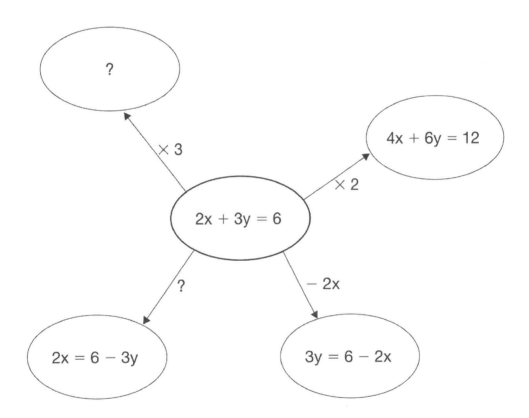

Children could be invited to fill in the blanks – whether inside the ellipses or to find the links.

The idea could be extended so that only the outside ellipses contain information, and the pupils have to deduce the centre of the spider.

Appendix 21 A writing frame for problem-solving

Understanding and representing the problem – recognising problem types and organising relevant information	I have to find out . . . The information I can use is . . .
Selecting or planning the solution – breaking the problem into steps and reviewing alternative strategies	The other information I have to find is . . . I will use . . . Any other calculations I need to make would be . . . I will present my results, using . . .
Executing the plan – carrying out routines, such as calculations	I found out that . . .
Evaluating results – reviewing and making sense of answers	I can check my answer by . . .

Appendix 22 Progression grids

Progression grid for problem-solving activities: a filled example for T total problem-solving activity (see www.youtube.com/watch?v=1v5BHn78Bak) and a blank version.

Representing	Analysing	Interpreting & Evaluating	Communicating & Reflecting
Clear choice of approach and appropriate form of representation	*Accurate results, working towards a solution identifying patterns*	*Explain or justifying findings and generalisations*	*Quality of written explanation*
Shows understanding of the task. Draws a number of Ts on a grid	Obtains some results for a number of Ts, including T totals and T numbers	Explains how to find a T total using the grid for a given T number	Makes a simple statement, such as the size of T total increasing as the T number does
Stores solutions so that they can easily be accessed	Obtains a number of results that enable them to talk about the patterns	Explains how to work out a T total given the T number without using a grid	Makes a statement explaining how the numbers in the T relate to the initial number (numerically)
Systematically lists solutions	Analyses solutions and uses them to make predictions	Identifies a word formula that can be used to find a T total given T number (or vice versa); explains how it was created	
Moves from recording data to developing a theoretical model that can be tested		Identifies algebraic relationship between T total and T number	Explains how the numbers in the T relate to the initial number (algebraically)
	Expands problem to consider rotations of T or other shapes (i.e. E or F)		Comments on how they produced their formula and demonstrate it working

PROGRESSION

	Representing	Analysing	Interpreting & Evaluating	Communicating & Reflecting
P R O G R E S S I O N				

References

Berger, A., Morris, D. and Portman, J. (2000) *Implementing the National Numeracy Strategy for Pupils with Learning Difficulties.* London: David Fulton.

Black, P. (1999) 'Assessment, Learning Theories and Testing Systems' in Murphy, P. (ed.) *Learners, Learning and Assessment*. London: The Open University (Paul Chapman Publishing).

Black, P. and Wiliam, D. (1998) *Inside the Black Box*. London: King's College.

Bloom, B.S. and Krathwohl, D. (1956) *Taxonomy of Educational Objectives: The Classification of Educational Goals.* Handbook 1: *Cognitive Domain*. New York: Addison Wesley.

Bruner, J. (1996) *The Culture of Education*. Cambridge, MA/London: Harvard University Press.

Buckley, S. and Bird, G. (1993) 'Teaching Children with Down's Syndrome to Read', *Down's Syndrome: Research & Practice* 2(2): 47–50.

Corbett, J. and Slee, R. (2000) 'An International Conversation on Inclusive Education' in Armstrong, F., Armstrong, D. and Barton, L. (eds.) *Inclusive Education: Policy, Contexts and Comparative Perspectives*. London: David Fulton.

DfE (2013a) National Curriculum in England: Framework for Key Stages 1 to 4, www.gov.uk/government/publications/national-curriculum-in-england-framework-for-key-stages-1-to-4

DfE (2013b) National Curriculum in England: Mathematics Programmes of Study – Key Stage 3, www.gov.uk/government/publications/national-curriculum-in-england-mathematics-programmes-of-study

DfE (2013c) National Curriculum in England: Mathematics Programmes of Study – Key Stages 1 and 2, www.gov.uk/government/publications/national-curriculum-in-england-mathematics-programmes-of-study

DfE (2014a) National Curriculum in England: Mathematics Programmes of Study – Key Stage 4, www.gov.uk/government/publications/national-curriculum-in-england-mathematics-programmes-of-study

DfE (2014b) Performance – P Scale – Attainment Targets for Pupils with Special Educational Needs, www.gov.uk/government/publications/p-scales-attainment-targets-for-pupils-with-sen

DfE (2014c) Statutory Guidance National Curriculum in England: Framework for Key Stages 1 to 4, www.gov.uk/government/publications/national-curriculum-in-england-framework-for-key-stages-1-to-4/the-national-curriculum-in-england-framework-for-key-stages-1-to-4

DfE (2015) Special Educational Needs and Disability Code of Practice: 0 to 25 Years, www.gov.uk/government/publications/send-code-of-practice-0-to-25

DfES (1999) *Framework for Teaching Mathematics – Reception to Year 6*. London: DfES Publications.

DfES (2001) *Framework for Teaching Mathematics – Years 7, 8 and 9*. London: DfES Publications.

DfES (2002) *Accessing the National Curriculum for Mathematics – Examples of What Pupils with Special Educational Needs Should Be Able to Do at Each P Level* (ref. DfES 0292/2002). London: DfES Publications.

Dweck (2007) *The New Psychology of Success.* New York: Ballantine Books.

Fox, G. and Halliwell, M. (2000) *Supporting Literacy and Numeracy: A Guide for Teaching Assistants*. London: David Fulton.

Greeno, J.G., Pearson, P.D. and Schonenfield, A.H. (1997) 'Achievement and Theories of Knowing and Learning' in McCormick, R. and Paechter, C. (eds.) *Learning and Knowledge*. London: The Open University (Paul Chapman Publishing).

Hart, S. (2000) *Thinking through Teaching*. London: David Fulton.

Kay, J. and Yeo, D. (2003) *Dyslexia and Maths*. London: David Fulton.

Lave, J. and Wenger, E. (1991) *Situated Learning: Legitimate Peripheral Participation*. Cambridge: Cambridge University Press.

Lever, M. (2003) *Activities for Children with Mathematical Learning Difficulties: Number, Shape and Space, Measures and Handling Data*. London: David Fulton.

Lorenz, S. (1998) *Children with Down's Syndrome.* London: David Fulton.

MacGrath, M. (1998) *The Art of Teaching Peacefully.* London: David Fulton.

McNamara, S. and Moreton, G. (1997) *Understanding Differentiation: A Teacher's Guide*. London: David Fulton.

Mason, J.H. (1988) *Learning and Doing Mathematics.* Basingstoke/London: Macmillan.

Murphy, P. (1998) 'Supporting Collaborative Learning: a Gender Dimension' in Murphy, P. (ed.) *Learners, Learning and Assessment*. London: The Open University (Paul Chapman Publishing).

Ollerton, M. (2003) *Everyone Is Special*. Derby: Association of Teachers of Mathematics.

Prestage, S. and Perks, P. (2001) *Adapting and Extending Secondary Mathematics Activities: New Tasks for Old*. London: David Fulton.

Rogoff, B. (1998) 'Cognitive Development through Social Interaction: Vygotsky and Piaget' in Murphy, P. (ed.) *Learners, Learning and Assessment*. London: The Open University (Paul Chapman Publishing).

UNISON, NAHT, NET and Maximising Teaching Assistants (2016) *Professional Standards for Teaching Assistants*. Haywards Heath: NAHT Publications.

Vygotsky, L.S. (1962) *Thought and Language*. Cambridge, MA: MIT Press.

Wiske, M.S. (1998) 'What Is Teaching for Understanding?' in M.S. Wiske (ed.) *Teaching for Understanding. Guide: Linking Research with Practice*. San Francisco, CA: Jossey-Bass.

Index

Printed in Great Britain
by Amazon

67316835R00115